THE DEFENCE OF NORFOLK

1793–1815

John Barney

Mintaka Books

Published in the year two thousand by
Mintaka Books
30, Friars Quay, Norwich, Norfolk, NR3 1ES
Tel 01603 612815
Fax 01603 614667

Origination, printing and binding by
Witley Press Limited, Hunstanton, Norfolk, PE36 6AD

British Library Cataloguing in Publication Data
A catalogue record for this book is available from the British Library

ISBN 0 95378 091 0

Contents

Maps

Illustrations
between pages 40 and 41

Two members of the Norwich Rifle Corps, *E. Bell after Robert Dixon*

Colonel John Harvey, Norwich Light Horse, *John Opie*

Colonel John Patteson, Norwich Battalion, *William Beechey*

Badge of Diss Light Infantry
Shooting prize badge – Norwich Battalion

Jacket of a private in the East Norfolk Militia

West Norfolk militia private c. 1808

West Norfolk militia drummer c. 1800

Volunteers drilling on Cromer marrams, 1798, *Engraving by J. Walker after an original drawing by C. Catton junior.*

All illustrations except the last courtesy of Norfolk Museums Service (Norwich Castle Museum and Royal Norfolk Regimental Museum). The engraving of volunteers drilling at Cromer by courtesy of Cromer Town Council.

Preface

My interest in Norfolk's participation in the Napoleonic wars began when studying the relationships between the town of King's Lynn and the gentry of the surrounding countryside. This had led me to the correspondence held in the Norfolk Record Office of the Hamond and Folkes families, both of which at different times contributed officers to the regular army, the militia and the volunteers. I soon discovered that to do any justice to the theme it was necessary to consider the whole of the county, and to dig into the political background far enough to uncover the motives that made some enthusiastic soldiers from the very first and some to hang back until real danger, public pressure or actual compulsion forced them into service. Moreover it was desirable to consider just how much danger in fact surrounded the county, how the professional soldiers planned to defend against any possible landing, and how useful the numerous amateurs who sprang to arms were likely to have been had the worst occurred. The result is this book.

To make the text more readable I have confined information regarding my documentary sources to an appendix but it seems only right to acknowledge here the essential contribution made to any work of this kind by the usually anonymous correspondents, now long dead, to the local newspapers of the day, in this instance mainly *The Norfolk Chronicle*. My thanks are due to them and to certain army staff officers of that time, but also to Ian O'Brien, David Higgins and Richard Wilson who each read and commented on the text in its early stages of preparation; to Terry Burchell who photographed pictures and artifacts to provide certain of the illustrations; to Kate Thaxton and Norma Watt of the Norfolk Museums Service; to Philip Judge who redrew the maps from my rough drafts; and to the staff of the Norfolk Record Office in Norwich and of the Public Record Office in Kew.

John Barney
September 2000

1. The Threat of Invasion

In 1805 Britain was in grave danger of an invasion, a danger as great as any between the Spanish Armada of 1588 and Hitler's plans in 1940 for Operation Sealion. Invasion alarms had occurred in most wars of the eighteenth century, and not without justification. Between 1744 and 1783 Britain was at least three times under threat of an invasion by the French. In 1744 a French expedition commanded by the famous Marshall Saxe was poised for a surprise attack on Essex but was aborted after a violent storm wrecked the vessels and ruined the stores collected at Dunkirk. Between 1756 and 1759 a French army was encamped near the coast ready to embark but unable to sail due to the vigilance of the British blockade and the eventual defeats of French fleets by Boscawen at Lagos and by Hawke at Quiberon Bay. In the summer of 1779 and again in 1781 the combined fleets of the French and Spanish were in effective control of the Channel but ultimately achieved nothing although troops were available for an attempt. In none of these periods did Britain have at home either an army sufficient in numbers to oppose the potential invader in the field with any certainty of success or fortifications adequate to protect its major cities or its all-important dockyards. From 1757 the militia was reorganised to provide a modest home army in time of war but the civil population remained otherwise largely unmoved. The possibility of wild highlanders in London in 1745 caused some panic in the provinces and a run on the Bank of England, but nothing was done at any time to arm or train the general populace to fight the French. Indeed the aristocratic government would probably have found such a prospect rather more alarming than an invasion itself.

When the next French wars began in 1793 home defence was no better organised. For the next three years the main military concern of the government at home was to secure against internal unrest or even revolution. Thereafter, with an actual invasion attempt on Ireland frustrated in December 1796 solely by weather, the possibility of an invasion of Britain itself loomed ever larger, especially in 1797/98 and again for some months in 1801. Britain never lost command of the sea during these wars, although the fleet was for a while paralysed in 1797 when many seamen mutinied, but such command was never absolute when ships were powered only by sail. Gales could drive a blockading squadron away from its station and allow the ships in the blockaded harbour to escape before their opponents could regain station. Adverse winds or calms could neutralise a defending fleet for crucial days giving time for a bold raid with oared light craft or even a full scale invasion.

The most dangerous period of all began when the war broke out again in May 1803 after the thirteen months of the uneasy Peace of Amiens. From the first Napoleon's declared plan was of an invasion of England and for over two years his Army of England gathered in the Pas de Calais and in the immediate hinterland of Boulogne with more troops only a few days march away available as waves of reinforcements. The harbour of Boulogne itself and

1

those of three smaller ports, also to the west of Cap Gris Nez, were fortified, improved and greatly enlarged. Fleets of barges and gunboats were built along the coast from Friesland to Brittany and assembled in those harbours. The larger vessels were sail powered, not handy, but capable with fair winds of covering the thirty miles to the English shores on a single tide. The smaller were powered by oars, and thus independent of winds given gentle summer weather. Their combined capacity was calculated to land 167,000 men in England over the course of three days.

Admiral Jervis's boast, "I do not say the French will not come. I only say they will not come by sea." might have proved hollow in the right circumstances of weather, which could have allowed the Brest squadron to escape to form a temporary shield for the invasion fleet, even at the cost of a crushing naval defeat. But to set out without any support at all from a covering fleet would have been a gamble on weather and the chance of some temporary absence of the defending squadrons. A night assault, still more risky, would surely have been beyond the capability of those navigating the awkward landing craft. Even had a landing been effected without defeat on the beaches, the possibility remained that the force ashore might be cut off in England by British reassertion of sea command. Napoleon, a brilliant strategist, was also a gambler and a lucky one, but sufficiently realistic to appreciate that at least temporary sea command was essential. Here he was failed by his admirals who lacked either the skill, the imagination or just the luck to escape from the several blockades, combine and, as was planned, circumnavigate the British Isles to join with the Dutch and hold the Channel narrows while the invasion fleet made its crossing. Eventually their main fleet was destroyed at Trafalgar but before that Napoleon had given up, forced through Britain's successful diplomacy to march his army east to fight the Austrians and Russians. He never totally abandoned invasion plans; as late as 1813 he was driving his naval commanders forward in a campaign to outbuild the British navy, combining new French ships with more available from his allies and clients in the Netherlands, Genoa and Venice. Only his conclusive defeats in Germany and Spain in 1813 and 1814 and the actual invasion of France brought those schemes to an end.

In contrast to apathy or over confidence in earlier wars, the British public in 1803/05 caught invasion fever. There had been alarm after 1796, but alarm turned to expectation in the summers of 1803, 1804 and 1805 when for the first time everyone in the kingdom must have been aware of invasion as a real possibility. Given the constraints imposed on the French by weather, tides and their choice of bases, England's military leaders and the local populations were perfectly clear that the area most threatened was Kent and East Sussex. A dispersal of French effort, either an intentional diversion or simply accidental, might bring invaders to Hampshire or north of the Thames estuary to Essex or Suffolk. With better prospects in the southeast of the country nearer London, Norfolk was an unlikely initial target for a main invading force. Although the navy used Yarmouth Roads as an anchorage and as an

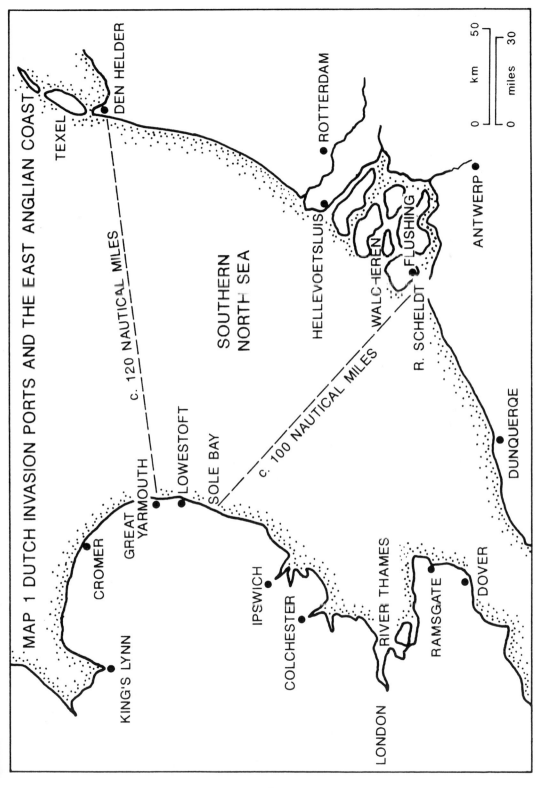

MAP 1 DUTCH INVASION PORTS AND THE EAST ANGLIAN COAST

TEXEL

DEN HELDER

ROTTERDAM

HELLEVOETSLUIS

WALCHEREN

FLUSHING

ANTWERP

R. SCHELDT

DUNQUERQE

SOUTHERN
NORTH SEA

c. 120 NAUTICAL MILES

c. 100 NAUTICAL MILES

LOWESTOFT

SOLE BAY

GREAT
YARMOUTH

CROMER

KING'S LYNN

IPSWICH

COLCHESTER

RIVER THAMES

RAMSGATE

DOVER

LONDON

km   50

miles   30

0

3

assembly point for naval expeditions, there was no permanent base or dockyard to form the object of an enemy raid. Nevertheless the Dutch coast and fleet came under French control early in the wars and Norfolk could easily have been chosen as a target for a diversionary expedition, perhaps transported by ships based at the Texel or from the ports in the river Scheldt. The invaders would have faced natural difficulties. Yarmouth is difficult of approach due to the off-lying banks; King's Lynn too far from the continent, inaccessible except at high tide, and having a winding and inhospitable entrance channel. The remaining Norfolk coast has some tempting beaches but little shelter for ships anchored off while the few harbours in the north are tidal and unsuitable for vessels of any considerable size. Yet a raid in force was a distinct possibility and Norfolk shared fully in the alarms at the time of the principal crises. The twin themes of this book are the contribution that Norfolk made to the manpower of the armies of the Crown and the measures taken or planned for the defence of the county itself.

2.   County Administration and The Means of Defence

In the eighteenth and early nineteenth century there was no single authority for county administration and little formal organisation for the civil governance of the county at all. Most local administration, including the whole system of relief for the poor, was the responsibility of individual parishes under the supervision of local magistrates. Magistrates of each of the thirty-two Norfolk hundreds, always chosen from the propertied classes, tended to act jointly in trying cases but there was no formal requirement for them to do so. All Norfolk magistrates – or such at any rate as cared to attend – gathered together for Quarter Sessions where important cases were usually tried and matters applicable to the county as a whole might be considered. The county itself was responsible for little more than maintenance of the gaol in Norwich castle and for certain bridges. Trustees administered turnpikes and commissioners were responsible for certain harbours and navigations. The corporate towns of Norwich, King's Lynn, Yarmouth and Thetford were very largely independent of the county and had their own courts.

In peacetime direct influence by the central government was exercised in the county in just two ways. Assize courts sat in Norfolk twice each year with sessions at Norwich and Thetford. It was the duty – often the only duty – of the high sheriff to organise the Assizes and empanel a Grand Jury from gentlemen holding land worth annually one hundred pounds or more but the judges came from the royal courts. Otherwise directions from central government, especially on matters concerned with defence, came to the lord lieutenant, himself a government appointee, and he was responsible for effecting these either on his own or through such deputy lieutenants as he appointed (subject to government approval of his candidates). The deputy lieutenants, rather numerous during the wars, were usually also magistrates and so a meeting of the lieutenancy was not dissimilar to Quarter Sessions, or for that matter an empanelled Grand Jury. The membership of each included and was largely confined to men of superior property in the county and their older sons. Even direct national taxation was assessed and administered through local bodies of commissioners while the officers and staff of H M Customs serving in the Norfolk ports, though administered from London, were appointed on the recommendation of local magnates.

The principal influence of the county on the central government was exercised through its members of Parliament. The county itself and the towns of Norwich, Lynn and Yarmouth each sent two members to Parliament, and while the electorate in each case was limited it was too large simply to be bought, even at Lynn where there were only some 300 electors. Norwich, Lynn and the county commonly sent men to Parliament from Norfolk families. Some of these members were of more than local importance while others, as well as some of the unsuccessful candidates in such elections as were disputed, played an important part in the organisation of local defence in the Napoleonic wars. In particular Thomas Coke of Holkham was a member for the county throughout the period, sharing the seat until 1797 with Sir John Wodehouse of Kimberley and later with Sir Jacob Astley of Melton Hall. In Lynn, where the corporation was influential in avoiding disputed elections, the members during the war years were Colonel the Honourable Horatio Walpole (to 1809), his son, also Horatio (from 1809), and Sir Martin Browne Folkes of Hillington. Norwich politics were complex with frequent disputed elections and a strong radical element. From 1784 to 1802 one of the city's two members was William Windham of Felbrigg, the only Norfolk politician of that period to rise to cabinet rank. Another, to his death in 1799, was the Honourable Henry Hobart, another from 1806 to 1812 was John Patteson and yet another, from 1812 to 1818, was Charles Harvey. All of those named had been, were or became amateur soldiers via the militia or the volunteers.

At Yarmouth, where the electorate has been described as both numerous and venal, there were several interests including those wielded by the Townshend and Harbord families but also naval influence and local factions. None of the several wartime members (most Yarmouth elections were contested and changes were frequent) were volunteer soldiers of note but one, William Loftus, was an officer in the regular army and two were naval officers. The four MPs who sat, two each, for the rotten borough of Castle Rising and the scarcely less rotten borough of Thetford were often strangers to the county, the nominees of the Howard and Walpole families at the former and of the Fitzroy dukes of Grafton or of the Catholic Lord Petre at the latter. Only two during the period of the wars were Norfolk natives. Robert Buxton, a local squire and ardent Pitt supporter, sat for Thetford in the Grafton interest to 1796 but declined to continue after the duke went into opposition. James Mingay, a Thetford born Whig and an eminent London barrister, was elected for Thetford in 1806 with Grafton support but was unseated shortly after on a charge of bribery. Neither of these men became soldiers.

The responsibility for the defence of the country as a whole rested ultimately with the King and his ministers and with the army's commander in chief to whom district military commanders were responsible. Norfolk lay within the Eastern Military District comprising northern Essex, Suffolk, Cambridge and Huntingdon as well as Norfolk, the district commander having his headquarters at Colchester. However military responsibility specifically for a county was delegated to its lord lieutenant. From 1792 until his death in 1807 the lord lieutenant of Norfolk was George, first Marquess Townshend of Raynham. Although the Townshend family were Whigs by tradition, the lord lieutenancy was not usually a party matter, and during his time in office Townshend, who took his duties very seriously, does not seem to have been influenced by party considerations in his recommendations for appointments of officers in the militia and volunteers or of the numerous wartime deputy lieutenants provided he was satisfied as to the overall loyalty and respectability of the candidates.

The army's approach to Norfolk's defence during these wars is dealt with in Chapter 4: in a time of extreme danger the War Office did not regard Norfolk as a matter of priority. The only force commanded by the lord lieutenant by virtue of his office was the county militia but this was not available to him in wartime. His and the county's responsibility for providing a militia and providing also the regular additional drafts of men that wartime legislation demanded are dealt with in Chapter 5 but the simple fact is that they were taken from their county to serve elsewhere. With Norfolk's own militia unavailable and with little more than token regular forces allocated to the county, local defence, if required, was by default a matter for voluntary effort. With foreign trade brought to a virtual standstill the war begun in 1793 was very far from popular, and especially not amongst the manufacturers, the merchants and the land-owning classes, the latter in particular being more concerned with the need in the aftermath of the French Revolution for greater internal security. There were strong strains of radicalism, not to say Jacobinism, running through the population, especially in Norwich, and riot or even revolution was what was feared. In the absence of adequate regular armed units which could act in support of the civil power there were calls for local volunteer forces.

Pure volunteer units, that is units raised entirely independently of the militia, seem to have been formed at all previous moments of national crisis especially when invasion seemed a possibility. Governments were inclined to be suspicious of any system which armed the populace without embodying them into disciplined units which could be made subject to central control, and had sore experience of the quasi-revolutionary Irish Volunteers of the American war to justify their suspicions. However the need was seen as great and enabling legislation, Pitt's Defence Act, was passed in early 1794. There was provision for two main types of volunteer force, yeomanry (cavalry) and infantry. Yeomanry were expected to supply their own horses and so were usually farmers and their sons, officered by land-owning gentry. Provided they agreed to serve in specified emergencies outside their home counties both types were entitled to pay for days spent in training and were to have arms provided by the government as well as either clothing or a clothing allowance although there were units which disdained to apply for any such assistance. The emphasis in the parliamentary discussion of these forces was on their role not in repelling an invasion but in maintaining the tranquillity of the country should an invasion be attempted. While the army and militia would confront the invaders, the volunteers would suppress any attempt at riot or insurrection in support of the enemy by disaffected persons at home. Unspoken was the general assumption that suppression of other riots, as in time of food shortages, could also be a duty of volunteer forces.

In Norfolk the war was even less popular than elsewhere with trade and shipping of the major towns and ports suffering heavily. Moreover Thomas Coke of Holkham, Foxite Whig, county MP and the largest landowner in the county, was strongly opposed to the war which carried much weight in western and northern Norfolk from whence he drew his strongest support.

However the other county MP, Sir John Wodehouse, was a government supporter in favour of Pitt and of the war, and others of the gentlemen of the Norfolk, whatever their political leanings, were not averse to setting up a force for local security. In late March 1794, when Pitt's Defence Bill was still passing through Parliament, Lord Townshend called a meeting of Norfolk landowners in London to consider raising a subscription for county defence. Held on the last day of March, this meeting was well attended by the principal nobles and landowners connected with the county and most of the county's MPs. However it proved to be about equally divided. There were some who were for raising a subscription there and then and proceeding to a call for volunteers. But others, led by Coke, held that on such a matter a public meeting should be called by the high sheriff and held within the county itself. Not only Coke but others including the duke of Norfolk took the constitutional point harking back to the seventeenth century that it was improper and illegal for the Crown to ask for private subscriptions to fund a public liability and by so doing avoid parliamentary scrutiny of the expenditure. In this they were echoing the opposition line in the debates on the Bill in Parliament itself. Eventually, while the meeting agreed that the greatest exertions were necessary for defence and that a further meeting in Norfolk itself was unavoidable, those opposing a subscription departed leaving the remainder putting their names to a preliminary subscription list.

The high sheriff for that year, John Dashwood of Cockley Cley, duly called a public meeting at the Shire House in Norwich for April 12. This was so well attended that many, even some "of the first quality" could not get in, the lord lieutenant himself having some difficulty. Townshend explained that the plan was to create units of yeomanry cavalry in every hundred and volunteer infantry in the coastal towns. He was confident that enough landowners would come forward to provide an officer corps and that subscriptions would be given generously. His cousin Charles and William Windham made speeches in support, the latter explaining that nobody would be required to march beyond the area he had agreed to when volunteering even "on the appearance of an invasion", words in the Bill which had alarmed some who felt them too wide and dangerously imprecise. The proposals met with considerable opposition led by Thomas Coke. He did not think the war justified and he greatly doubted any real danger of invasion, but above all he could not agree that a subscription was proper or legal. He found support from lawyer James Mingay but most reported speeches were for the proposals.

When the main resolutions were put to the meeting there was such confusion that the sheriff was unable to determine whether the resolutions had been passed or not. Eventually it was decided that those wishing to proceed with a subscription should adjourn elsewhere. At this adjourned meeting a committee "for the internal defence and security of the county" was created, and plans established, taking advantage of the new legislation, to form bodies of voluntary cavalry in the shire hundreds and companies of volunteer infantry in the towns. Meetings were to be held around the county at which volunteers could subscribe their names. The names of those to serve as officers were to be sent to the lord lieutenant for onward submission to the King. At the same meeting a defence fund was created to which anyone might subscribe. The fund, already begun in London, attracted many substantial subscriptions including £200 from Lord Townshend and £100 apiece from county landowners such as Lords Orford, Petre, Suffield, Walsingham and Walpole and from MPs including Windham, Hobart, Buxton and Charles Townshend. The duke of Norfolk, Coke, and influential Coke supporters Astley, Pratt and Hamond were names notably absent but by the end of May over £10,000 had been subscribed. The creation of the Norfolk volunteer units, which followed, is described in Chapter 6.

3. Norfolk's Senior Soldiers

At the beginning of the wars there were a few men in Norfolk who combined high social status with some military experience and who felt both a duty and a desire to take part in organising the military efforts of the county. The senior of these was the lord lieutenant himself, George Townshend. The Townshends had been prominent politically in Norfolk in the previous century and Charles, the second viscount, had risen to national eminence and cabinet rank as foreign secretary under George I and George II. However he fell out with his brother-in-law Robert Walpole, Norfolk's rising star who became the country's virtual prime minister, and retreated to his estates at Rainham for the remainder of his life. Thereafter and for some years Walpoles, becoming earls of Orford, were treated as Norfolk's premier family although the national political status of the Townshends was restored by the second viscount's brilliant grandson (George Townshend's younger brother) Charles who rose to become Chancellor of the Exchequer before his premature death in 1767.

George Townshend, born in 1724, had entered the army as a young man and had served under the duke of Cumberland at both Fontenoy and Culloden. By the time he succeeded as fourth viscount in 1764 he had behind him a military career of more than twenty years and held the rank of major general. In 1759 he had succeeded to the command of the British troops at Quebec after the death of Wolfe where he had negotiated the French surrender. He had also been MP for the county in which capacity he had been involved in promoting the reform of the militia.

Horace Walpole described him when a young man as having "...much address, some humour, no knowledge, great fickleness, greater want of judgement and with still more disposition to ridicule ...". In later years the same author referred to "...his proud, and sullen, and contemptuous temper..." However accurate that may be he certainly had a talent for upsetting people partly due to a hot temper and partly due to his considerable ability as a caricaturist. Shortly prior to his service in Canada he had challenged his neighbour, the ageing Lord Leicester, to a duel because of some slighting remarks the latter was said to have made about the militia in which Townshend at the time commanded a regiment. This challenge Lord Leicester politely declined in a famous letter, pointing out the absurdity of a contest between an elderly man unaccustomed to weapons and a much younger soldier. Fifteen years later Townshend took part in a notorious duel in which, firing first, he shot Lord Bellamont in the stomach.

Made Lord Lieutenant of Ireland in 1767 Townshend went with proposals for major reforms but his discretion was limited by British parliamentary obstruction while his initiatives became bogged down in the labyrinths of Irish politics of that time and he ended by pleasing nobody. The Victorian historian Lecky, writing of Townshend's time in Ireland, described him as "...by no means an unaimiable man. He was ... honest and frank; popular in his manners, witty, convivial, and with a great turn for caricature, but violent and capricious in his temper, and ... destitute of tact, dignity and decorum. He certainly drank hard, and he was accused of low vices, and a great love of low companions ...[being] ...generally thought a good-humoured, cheerful man, meaning no harm, disinterested, benevolent and sincere."

On his return to England in 1772 he lived partly in London and partly on his estates at Raynham. When in the closing stages of the American war an Act authorised the formation of volunteer units, he recruited a mixed troop of volunteer cavalry and riflemen for internal security and local defence in the event of invasion. His was the first such unit in Norfolk although in 1779 King's Lynn corporation had raised a company of volunteer infantry and an artillery company to man its fort on no legal authority but its own. Other Norfolk units followed Townshend's or were at least projected, one by Sir Edward Astley MP of Melton Hall and another by Lord Orford. Townshend's troop, which was christened The Norfolk Rangers, was only fully recruited and armed shortly before the peace of 1783, but the idea and the ambition to command local troops remained with its commander.

Townshend became lord lieutenant of Norfolk in 1792 following the death of the third earl of Orford. Although the breach between the Townshends and the Walpoles had been partially healed when both families had become involved in the reform of the militia in the 1750s, Townshend had been by no means certain that he would obtain the appointment. There were suggestions that the earl of Buckinghamshire, a member of an old Norfolk family, might be given the post through the influence with Pitt of his son then Major (later Colonel) Hobart, Tory MP for Norwich. The Townshends' Whig history might have been thought a handicap, but in due course George Townshend was appointed.

By the outbreak of war the military traditions of two other leading families of the county were absorbed in the militia with Colonels Walpole and Wodehouse, Whig and Tory respectively, commanding the counties two militia regiments (see Chapter 5). However the Honourable William Assheton Harbord, son of the first Lord Suffield of Gunton and husband of Caroline Hobart, was aged twenty-eight when Pitt's Defence Bill of 1794 provided the authority to create a number of temporary regular regiments to be known as fencibles. Some of these were infantry and some cavalry units, recruited for the duration of the war but for home service only as an additional defence against invasion and also for aid to the civil power in the event of riot or insurrection.

Harbord, fit and unemployed other than as MP for a Wiltshire rotten borough, set about to recruit a fencible regiment, the Norfolk Fencible Cavalry, in the early summer of 1794, the only such unit raised in Norfolk. He, of course, was to be commander, but its lieutenant colonel and second in command was Sir Jacob Astley. Astley had been a junior militia officer in the American war and, as a member of a Whig family and son of former county MP Sir Edward Astley, by his appointment nicely balanced the political interest in the regiment. Immediately after formation the new unit moved to Bury and then wintered in billets in the Lynn area. The following Spring it moved to Carlisle and was later in Edinburgh where in 1797 it took part in suppressing anti-militia riots. It remained in Scotland until 1800 when it returned to Norfolk to be disbanded at Dereham. Neither it nor the other fencible regiments were reactivated in 1803.

William Earle Bulwer of Heydon was a Norfolk landowner who at the outbreak of war was an army captain on half pay. He had begun his military career as a junior officer in the West Norfolk Militia during the American war. After the war ended he had become first a lieutenant in the 68th Foot and then from 1787 a captain in the 34th, transferring to half pay in 1792. There is no record that he was ever on active service. In the early stages of the new war, in a drive to increase the army by at least 25,000 men, a device was adopted of granting commissioned rank, or promotion in existing rank, to men who could raise entirely new units, their rank or increased rank depending on the size of the formation raised. Bulwer was just one of several who sought to take advantage of this opportunity for professional advancement.

He began by raising an independent company but, with support from the city, his ambitions grew so that by May 1794 he was advertising in the *Norfolk Chronicle* for recruits for a new regiment called provisionally the Norwich Royal Regiment of Volunteers. This enterprise met with success and he was promoted for his efforts first to major and then in September to lieutenant colonel. The regiment, once recruited, had but a short career. As the 106th Foot it moved to Waterford in Ireland in 1795 but by the end of that year it had been disbanded along with many other new regiments, such as those provided by the cities of Manchester, Birmingham, Bristol and Glasgow, to provide drafts to replenish older established units. Bulwer thus went back onto half pay but remained anxious to serve in any capacity suitable to his now advanced rank.

In the same year that Bulwer raised his regiment Colonel (later General) Loftus of Stiffkey, son-in-law to Lord Townshend, raised a regiment of cavalry which became the 24th Light Dragoons. It is unclear to what extent this was recruited in Norfolk, for it was eventually listed on the Irish establishment and few of the officers had names familiar amongst the Norfolk gentry, but it had a longer history than Bulwer's, lasting until it was disbanded in 1802. Indeed in 1804 the 27th Light Dragoons, originally raised in 1795, were renumbered as the 24th and Loftus became their colonel, although he does not appear to have gone abroad with them to the West Indies or to India where they remained until returning home in 1819 to be disbanded. Raising a regiment at that time was a form of financial speculation. The colonel, once having authority from the government to recruit, could sell commissions to officers for substantial sums and use the proceeds to recruit and equip the rank and file for whom, provided they passed inspection, there was a degree of government subsidy. A successful colonel could clear five thousand pounds or more on initial formation with one thousand men, but disaster threatened if enough fit recruits could not be obtained or they did not pass inspection as the subsidies would become repayable and were in any case less than the bounties which had to be paid.

In 1793 Norfolk had one regular soldier in residence, although holding no command, who had strong views on how Norfolk might be defended. This was General John Money. Money was born around 1741 of a Trowse family and inherited a small estate there. He entered the army via the Norfolk Militia in 1760, soon after transferring to the regulars as a cornet in Elliot's Light Dragoons. He was present at the battle of Fellinghausen in 1761 and in a number of further minor actions in the closing stages of the Seven Years War. By February 1770 he had become a captain in the 9th Foot and went with that regiment to Canada. There he took part in Burgoyne's expedition of 1777 south towards New York serving on the staff as quartermaster general. A rumour reached Norfolk that he had been killed in Burgoyne's last action but this was untrue and he was taken prisoner in September when the entire expeditionary force surrendered at Saratoga. It is possible that he was exchanged and came home before the war's end in 1783 as many years later he referred to a survey he had made of south coast defences in 1780.

After the war he went on half pay and never again joined the active list of the British Army although he continued to the end of his life to receive promotions by brevet notwithstanding his half pay status. He became lieutenant colonel in 1790; full colonel in 1795; major general in 1798; lieutenant general in 1805; and full general in 1814. Meanwhile he became an active if controversial figure in Norwich society. Above Trowse he built the first house at Crown Point, named after a fort which Burgoyne's expedition had passed on their way south to Saratoga. There he held annual balls, one of which is referred to in William Windham's diary. He farmed several hundred acres and although this was but a small estate as compared to those of the major Norfolk landowners it had a "park" where he conducted experiments with artillery in 1804/5.

He never married but, according to Rye's *Norfolk Families*, had three acknowledged illegitimate children. Rye's informant, a General Harvey, told him that, "He had by the Hon Miss Fraser, sister to General Fraser, who was betrothed to him but never married and died in childbirth, a son, Lieutenant Colonel [in fact Lieutenant General] Archibald Money CB of 11th Dragoons who died 1858". This man is buried at Trowse Newton. His tomb in the churchyard confirms the date of death and gives his age then as eighty. From this it seems his birth was in 1778 suggesting that his conception, if not birth, must have taken place in Canada where Money had been stationed since 1771. Elizabeth Gurney wrote in her journal after meeting him that despite his acknowledged charm, "It is better to overlook such people as him who are so fasenating and not good characters …".

He never lost interest in military matters and in 1785 was experimenting with balloons making two ascents from Norwich. On his second ascent on 22 July an "improper wind" blew him out to sea. He came down in the water and spent several hours clinging to the wreckage before being rescued by a Revenue cutter. In 1787 he became involved in a mysterious conflict with a former friend Sir Thomas Beevor of Hethel, conducted in published letters in which each accused the other of libel, although what was contained in the original unpublished paper, the subject of the dispute, is unclear. A self-styled impartial pamphlet on the affair, published by the printer who had received the original paper, implies that Money was well known for seeking publicity as well as for being a ladies man, but does nothing to heal the dispute or explain what in substance it was about. In his conclusion the author asks rhetorically "Is it not notorious to the most superficial observer, that upon every occasion which has offered, he has *endeavoured* to distinguish himself? ...can Mr M demonstrate that he hath observed an unsinning obedience to the various duties of his station? Can he boast a life unsullied by actions which morality would condemn?"

Between 1790 and the end of 1792 Money, despairing of further military employment in Britain, had an adventurous career on the continent, first offering his services to the rebel party in the Austrian Netherlands. This rebellion had begun in 1789 as a reaction by an uneasy alliance of right and left wing Belgians, the latter inspired by the events in France, against sweeping reforms in administration imposed by the Austrian Emperor Joseph II. Having raised a volunteer force in the Netherlands the rebels invaded the Austrian territories and achieved a surprise success, driving the Austrian troops into Luxembourg and taking control of the country. But by the time Money joined their army, when he was given the rank of major general and placed in command of some five thousand men, the rebels had fallen out amongst themselves and the country was descending into anarchy. A reconquest by Austrian troops began in late 1790 finding the defending forces in disarray and half-hearted. Money was involved in one sharp engagement at Tirlemont but then had to join in the general retreat on Brussels which fell to the Austrians in early December. The revolution was over.

On returning home Money had offered to raise a corps of 1,000 men to serve in India against Hyder Ali but the offer was refused by the government. His next service was in 1792 after he was invited in the spring of that year to raise a legion for the French army after the National Assembly had passed a decree allowing four foreign generals to be taken into service. He was still in Paris on the night of 9 August 1792, when he was wakened with the news that the mob were about to attack the Tuilleries intending to massacre the royal family. He and an aide went at once to the palace finding the streets empty despite the noise of drums beating to arms. Once there they went to the royal apartments where nearly one hundred officers were gathered. It was not until early morning that they learned that the King had gone to the Assembly for protection. Money followed to the Assembly but could not gain admission, so after taking off his epaulettes, he returned to Paris. There he found the streets crowded and saw a mob carrying on pikes and bayonets the heads of the Swiss Guards who had been butchered at the Tuilleries after he had left.

15

Between August and December Money was part of the French army engaged in defending the country against its invasion by Austria and Prussia in support of the monarchy. When the invasion began the French army was commanded by Lafayette but he was promptly removed and replaced by Dumouriez. After initial reverses the latter joined his army with another commanded by Kellerman and in September they succeeded in holding off the Austrians at the battle of Valmy. When the Austrians retreated Dumouriez marched north on a counter offensive into Flanders and in mid November attacked the Austrians who had gone into winter quarters, defeating them at the battle of Jemappes. The French then moved on to capture Brussels. The *Norfolk Chronicle* for 5 January 1793 contains the following:

> Extract from a letter from General Money at Bruxelles to a friend in Norwich dated December 23, 1792.
>
> I arrived here last night from the army, and this morning I sent in my resignation to the Commissaries of the Constituent Assembly. It was always my intention to have quitted as soon as the campaign was over. I see by the public papers here, that England is arming, and the militia is called out. God forbid, I should ever have been in arms against my country; on the contrary, I would be the first man to draw my sword in defence of its happy constitution. I am offered the command of the Brabant army by General Dumouriez, with the rank of a Lieutenant-General – a brilliant situation for a military man – but which I have refused as nothing can induce me to serve now. I could not with honour have resigned during the campaign, or with safety have quitted the army, without the certainty of having been either assassinated by the people before I could have got out of France, or by the troops immediately under my command.
>
> When I engaged to serve these people they had a King and a Constitution, now they have neither – they are all mad, and the army thinks so – if they were left to themselves a civil war amongst them would very soon ensue. My resignation has been accepted, and I shall be off to England in a few days.

Back at home Money volunteered to return to France on a diplomatic mission to attempt to save the life of King Louis but his suggestion, which hardly sounds practicable, was turned down and shortly after the king's execution the war with France began. Thereafter he returned to Norwich and turned his attention to writing a history of the 1792 campaign and in considering how best Norfolk might be defended should invasion occur. Never shy of expressing his opinions, and aware that he was the only senior soldier in the county with recent practical military experience, he continued throughout the wars to bombard Townshend and ministers of the government, in letters and in published pamphlets, with his views on military matters. These related variously to Norfolk, to the use or misuse of cavalry, to the need for units of irregulars and riflemen, to the use of balloons or prefabricated towers of his own design for purposes of observation, to the building of entrenched camps for the purpose of defending London, and to novel means of mounting mobile artillery. In most cases his advice sounds good; in nearly all it was ignored.

4. Plans for Defence

With most of the regular army abroad garrisoning colonies, conquering new ones or held for the various continental forays of those wars, and with the likely scene of any major invasion elsewhere, it is clear that even in times of the greatest danger the army command did not accord Norfolk much priority. The normal wartime establishment was one regiment at Yarmouth, another perhaps at King's Lynn, and a third plus two troops of cavalry at Norwich. Two out of three of these regiments were likely to be militia. In June 1795 the regiment at Lynn was the 38th Foot, just returned from campaigning on the continent, much reduced by casualties, and using Lynn more as a base for rest and recuperation than as a defensive post.

Norfolk did not at this time serve as the permanent base for any regular regiment although, when stationed in Norwich in 1783 while rebuilding its strength after captivity in America, the veteran 9th Regiment of Foot, the direct ancestor of the Royal Norfolk Regiment, had been authorised to expand its name to the 9th East Norfolk Regiment as an aid in local recruiting. However the days of formal county affiliations lay a century ahead and the regiment had neither a permanent depot in the county nor a second reserve battalion to remain in the area for recruiting purposes. It was recuperating in Norwich again in 1796 after a spell in the fever-ridden West Indies and in 1799 briefly rested in the city amongst the many other troops returned from the abortive campaign in North Holland. These had been landed at Yarmouth and were then temporarily billeted there or in Norwich. The 9th Foot took its opportunity on both occasions to recruit. Later it (and probably other regular units) sent recruiting parties into the county in the perennial need to rebuild ranks depleted by disease, desertion and casualties.

In August 1804, with most of his 18,000 troops, mainly militia, strung out between Woodbridge in the north-east and Warley Camp near Brentwood in the south-west, General Sir James Craig in command of the Eastern Military District had one weak regiment of regulars (467 men of the 24th Foot) and one regiment of dragoon cavalry (580 men of the 1st Dragoons) at Norwich; one larger regiment of militia (939 men of the Shropshire Militia) at Yarmouth; and nothing at all at that stage at Lynn. The only field artillery was one troop of light guns stationed at Norwich. By that time there was adequate barrack accommodation in both Yarmouth and Norwich for these forces in contrast to Ipswich, Woodbridge and Colchester where a massive programme of barrack building had been put in hand to accommodate the far larger forces stationed there. Except in times of obvious danger and even when accommodated in barracks the poorly paid soldiery were far from popular, being guilty, or at least believed to be guilty, of many acts of robbery and violence.

As early as 1794 General Money had pointed out to Townshend the dangers of an enemy seizing either or both of the "islands" of Lothingland and Flegg; Yarmouth must then fall and Norwich would be in the greatest danger.

He thought that field fortifications could be built between Aldeby and Haddiscoe and between Reedham and Wroxham to isolate any invaders who succeeded in effecting a bridgehead behind the rivers Bure and Waveney. His appreciation was seconded by that of an unnamed author of a staff paper of 1798 who identified Haddiscoe and Acle as key positions to be held in strength should Yarmouth fall, with Reedham as an intermediate post to defend the river passage and Wroxham as an alternative defensive position should the enemy land in the Happisburgh area. At that time there was no bridge over the Bure at Yarmouth so that the bridges at St Olave's, Acle and Wroxham, at all of which places there were extensive marshes, were the only means whereby an enemy force based at Yarmouth could approach Norwich. A defensive position at Haddiscoe, linked with another on Aldeby windmill hill, was thought equally important if the enemy should land further south and approach Yarmouth or Norwich from Beccles.

The assumption that Yarmouth could not be held in face of a direct assault from the sea was supported by a staff paper prepared by one Major Thomas Reynolds of the 30th Foot who surveyed and reported on the eastern region coastal defences in 1797. He envisaged two scenarios. In the first the enemy engaged in a raid solely on Yarmouth to destroy shipping and sack or ransom the town, bringing some 15,000 men. His paper ignored possible naval defences and assumed that the invaders would approach Yarmouth Roads on an easterly wind which would allow them access through the offlying sands by the St Nicholas Channel which lay roughly opposite the town. In his opinion the only part of the fixed defences which would prove of much value in opposing the intruders' vessels would be the small battery on the heights at Gorleston. This he advocated should be increased in power and made into a proper fort for 1,000 men.

There were four further and more heavily armed batteries along the Yarmouth shore from the harbour mouth northwards but Reynolds doubted their value. Ships entering and anchoring in the Roads would be out of effective range of any of them. With their guns pointing directly seawards they were ill-sited to enfilade the beach during an actual landing from boats. They hardly covered the north end of the beach at all being too far from Caister Heights; and their defensive ditches inevitably became choked with sand. Given that a landing could not be prevented, even if the batteries were manned as he supposed by 1,000 seamen volunteers from the ships in the harbour, the only hope of a successful defence lay, Reynolds postulated, in blocking the gates of the town itself with carts chained together. The narrow alleys within should also be blocked and the walls and town should be defended for as long as possible by such regular troops or militia as could be found – he hoped for up to 3,000 called from a camp to be established at Hopton Heath on Lothingland – and as many of the town's inhabitants as could be mustered to defend their property. For the use of the latter he recommended that 5,000 stand of arms be held in the town.

His second scenario assumed an invasion with 30,000 men to capture and

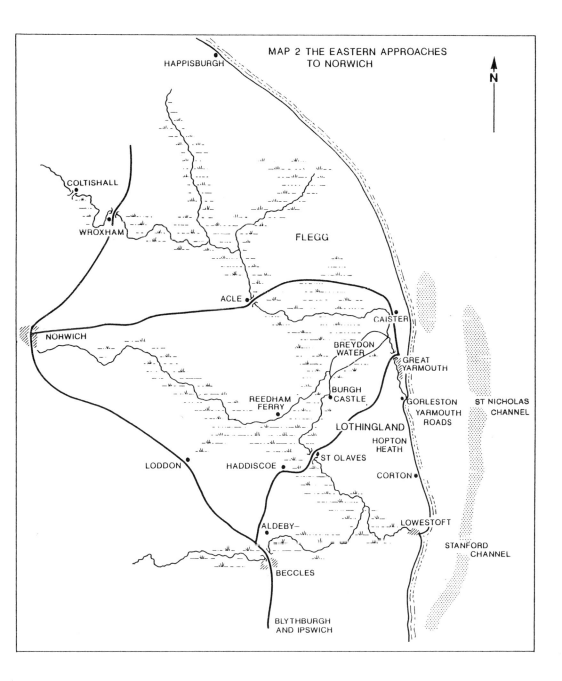

MAP 2 THE EASTERN APPROACHES
TO NORWICH

N

HAPPISBURGH

COLTISHALL

WROXHAM

FLEGG

ACLE

CAISTER

NORWICH

BREYDON
WATER

GREAT
YARMOUTH

BURGH
CASTLE

REEDHAM
FERRY

GORLESTON
YARMOUTH
ROADS

ST NICHOLAS
CHANNEL

LOTHINGLAND

HOPTON
HEATH

LODDON

HADDISCOE

ST OLAVES

CORTON

ALDEBY

LOWESTOFT

STANFORD
CHANNEL

BECCLES

BLYTHBURGH
AND IPSWICH

21

hold Norwich, whether as a diversion from a larger attack in the south or as a bargaining counter. This larger force would enable simultaneous landings at Yarmouth and at Corton, the vessels for the latter entering through the shallower Stanford Channel opposite Lowestoft. There were batteries at Lowestoft, better sited than those at Yarmouth but far from impregnable and hardly capable of resisting a determined onslaught. Reynolds considered that no force likely to be available on Lothingland could successfully defend both Lowestoft and Yarmouth and that enemy cavalry could soon drive them from Lothingland itself. In such circumstances the enemy would overrun both Lothingland and Flegg while the defending forces must either retreat over the bridge at St Olave's or throw themselves into the ruins of Burgh Castle to be evacuated by water. It was following such a reverse for the defenders that the positions at Haddiscoe and Acle in particular would become of significance. To man these and also to prevent an enemy at Lowestoft breaking out to the south Reynolds envisaged that more numerous forces from the south would need to march north, initially to Beccles. He acknowledged that should a subsidiary enemy force land first at Sole Bay the position to the north would be unpleasantly complicated.

Nothing was done in the first phase of the war to implement any of Reynolds' suggestions or to modify the Yarmouth forts. It must be remembered that Yarmouth was at the time a naval base of some importance, especially given the hostility of the Dutch under Napoleon's control, and the higher command seem to have assumed that the Navy would be able to destroy any invading squadron that reached the Yarmouth Roads. However the Navy does not appear to have regarded this task as a high priority, ships being most usually occupied in patrolling and blockading the continental coast. Naval suggestions for the defence of Yarmouth in the absence of their ships were confined to a proposal that in the face of an attack the buoys marking the ship channels through the sands should be removed. General Money was not the only person to remark that numerous Dutch skippers must already know these channels well enough without buoys.

When the second phase of the war began in 1803 rather more attention was paid to the question of Norfolk's defence although with much the same results. Sir James Craig, although understandably concentrating his limited resources in Essex and south Suffolk where a landing would be easier and could threaten London, sent one Major Bryce in November to survey the coast north from Yarmouth for feasible landing places and to recommend defensive works if required. In addition to the Yarmouth batteries the fortifications in the county were then confined to a battery at Cromer dating from the American war, which commanded the roadstead but not the beach, and the much older fort at Lynn. Responsibility for the maintenance of these installations lay with the towns themselves although the cannon, themselves usually old, were the property of the Ordnance Department.

Bryce thought that only a few places would present attractive landing to an enemy and, in particular, doubted the feasibility of Weybourne beach as far

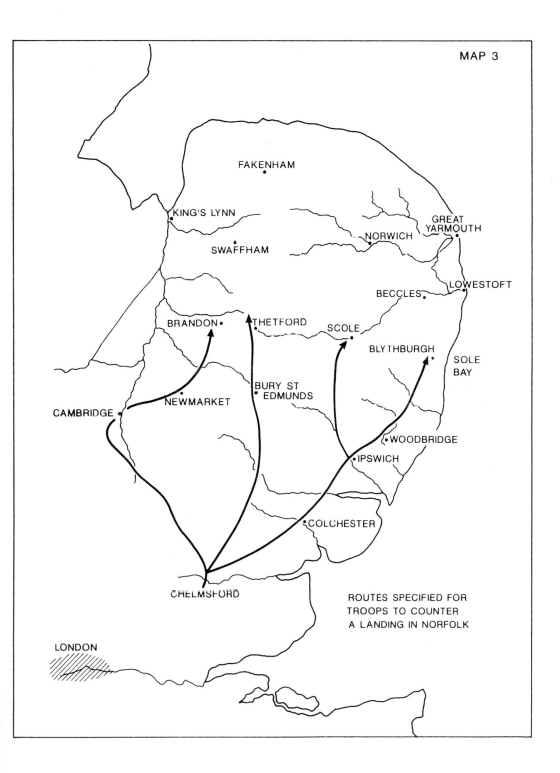

MAP 3

FAKENHAM

KING'S LYNN

GREAT
YARMOUTH

NORWICH

SWAFFHAM

LOWESTOFT

BECCLES

BRANDON

THETFORD

SCOLE

BLYTHBURGH

SOLE
BAY

BURY ST
EDMUNDS

NEWMARKET

CAMBRIDGE

WOODBRIDGE

IPSWICH

COLCHESTER

CHELMSFORD

ROUTES SPECIFIED FOR
TROOPS TO COUNTER
A LANDING IN NORFOLK

LONDON

too exposed to weather despite the presence of deep water close to the shore. He believed that flooding the marshes would be more effective than any other method of defence along much of the north and north-eastern coast but left it to locals to investigate how this might best be done. He recommended two small batteries at Cromer which could overlook the beach and another at Mundesley, but there principally to train the local sea fencibles in the use of cannon. Sea fencibles were auxiliary corps recruited from inshore fishermen and longshoremen who held protections from being pressed into the navy, officered by regular naval officers and engaged to serve for the duration either afloat or ashore for coastal defence. Bryce also recommended as many as three batteries for Holkham Bay and others at Blakeney, to guard the anchorage at the Pit, at Wells, and at Burnham. He was unable to inspect the coast beyond Hunstanton due to persistent fog but could see no object for an enemy in venturing as far as Lynn while, due to the extensive coastal marshes, the north-west of the county was mainly impractical for a landing. Any danger west of Holkham could best be countered with field artillery.

Bryce's report confirmed Craig in his pre-existing opinion that " [the enemy] is not likely to direct his attention to the coast of Norfolk north of Yarmouth." However he seconded the proposal of two guns for Mundesley in case a distressed enemy vessel should seek refuge and had already sent four carronades to Cromer to arm two new batteries there which could cover the beach although more to placate public opinion than because he believed there was any danger. He thought some mobile field artillery would be most use to cover the north coast, troops of four guns at each of Cley and Wells, to be manned by sea fencibles and moved by horses to be found locally or even by manpower alone. Alternatively, if placing artillery in the hands of amateurs was not approved, he wanted a regular artillery brigade at Holt and had told the local commander in Norwich to arrange for transport which in an emergency could convey the foot regiment there to the coast in support of the local volunteers.

Craig himself made a tour of the district in March 1804 but did not change his opinion that little danger was to be feared north of Yarmouth although he admitted that some vessels from a dispersed invasion fleet might come there accidentally. The coast was too far from the Continent for small craft to make a sudden raid and there were scarcely any points where larger transports could lie in shelter during a landing. The only decent landing place with some shelter and not separated from open country by cliff or marsh was Holkham Bay and he thought even that too far from any useful enemy objective. Locals at Mundesley and at Weybourne were convinced that their beaches were prime targets but Craig was sceptical. He approved the siting of the new guns at Cromer but as regards the northern ports observed that mounting heavy guns on sand dunes or shingle was likely to prove ineffective. Moreover the guns would have to be served by local sea fencibles. These were numerous enough but not necessarily available when wanted as they would usually be employed at sea. Moreover they could hardly be trusted to put up a firm defence against a determined attack when posted on isolated sandbars as would be the case at Wells and elsewhere. He continued to believe that field artillery would be more effective than any fixed positions although he did not in fact have any to spare. He repeated his request for a mixed brigade of 12 pounder field guns and howitzers to be based at Holt, but probably never obtained them as artillerymen were in short supply.

Yarmouth was a different matter. It could well be the object of an attack but Craig thought that a naval defence was the only real hope and had asked that the Navy hold more ships there. He condemned the existing batteries as useless but thought that modifying them or building fieldworks on the sandy shore was a hopeless proposition. It is significant that the earliest Eastern Region orders of August 1803 to deal with a possible Norfolk invasion consist of route plans to march forces from Colchester and Suffolk to Blythborough, to Scole, to Cambridge, or to Brandon, to interpose between the invaders and London rather than attempting to defend the coastline or even Norwich. Admittedly these plans were made before the build-up of local volunteer forces but it shows the way the military mind saw the problem. When from 1805 an entirely new chain of fortifications was built along the southern and eastern coasts of England, the Martello towers which can still be seen along the coasts of Suffolk and Essex, the northern end of the chain was at Aldeburgh, well south of Norfolk. A proposal to build more along the Yarmouth seafront to replace the shore batteries was put to Craig who thought a minimum of four would be needed and the benefit not worth the cost even though he repeated his condemnation of the existing batteries. Once again the security of Yarmouth was placed in the not over-eager hands of the navy. With so much potential danger elsewhere, it is clear that the higher command was not wasting too much time or money on Norfolk.

5. The Militia

In earlier generations the militia, or its predecessors such as the trained bands, had been organised purely for the local defence of the area in which they were raised. However from 1757 the militia had been reorganised on a quite different basis. Some 30,000 men were to be recruited in England with each county having a quota of men which it must raise and train. Norfolk's quota was approximately one thousand. In the event of war the regiments of all counties came under the authority of the central government to be deployed wherever in Britain (but not overseas) they might be required. Militia officers, for whom there was a substantial property qualification, held the King's commission, although appointed solely on the recommendation of the lord lieutenant of their county. The purpose of this property qualification was to ensure that the militia, like the regular army where most commissions were available only by purchase, remained under the control of men with a stake in maintaining the established, property based, order of society. Because the regular army which could be retained at home was clearly inadequate in numbers should invasion occur, the militia was called up in late 1792 even prior to the outbreak of war and remained embodied as a full time force through to the conclusion of the wars except for the brief period of peace, April 1802 to May 1803 under the Treaty of Amiens.

To find the rank and file of the militia each parish was allotted a proportion of its county's quota for selection primarily by ballot. However any person selected might obtain exemption by paying a substantial fine or might find and pay a substitute to serve in his stead. Parishes themselves might provide substitutes at a cost to be charged to the rates rather than see a man selected whose family would be left as a charge on the parish during his absence. Insurance clubs were formed, the members of which paid in a subscription to be used to purchase a substitute should any one of the members be caught by the ballot. The net result was that the militia rank and file tended to consist of poor men unable to afford a fine or of substitutes for others whose services had been purchased by a private or parish bounty. Not surprisingly the whole system was unpopular with those who could not avoid service under a system which, if not outright conscription, was certainly one of effective compulsion. There were anti-ballot riots in several places during the course of the wars, including especially Scotland when the militia ballot was extended to that country in 1797.

Norfolk was early associated with the militia reform. George Townshend himself was the MP who had introduced the bill in 1756 which reorganised the militia, and it was the two combined regiments of the new Norfolk Militia, under the command of the eccentric earl of Orford, which was the first militia unit to serve outside its home county in 1759 when it was marched to man the Hilsea lines at Portsmouth after a review before the King in Hyde Park. The militia, however unpopular with the rank and file, became a valued outlet for the energies of some of the younger members of the greater Norfolk families who served as the more senior officers. In late 1792, when first embodied ahead of the threatened war, there were two regiments each with some 500 men, the Eastern commanded by Colonel John Wodehouse of Kimberley, and the Western, commanded by Colonel the Honourable Horatio Walpole. Both regiments had other well known county names amongst their officers.

It was not only usual for a county's militia to serve outside the home county but actual policy. It was thought that desertion would be less if a regiment served at a distance from its origins while its soldiers would be less reluctant to act against civilians of a different part of the country, should that be necessary, than to act against their friends and neighbours. Regular moves of station were also policy to keep the regimental organisations on their toes and the men fit to march. Thus shortly after assembling at their depots, Yarmouth for the Eastern Regiment and Dereham for the Western, both regiments were marched away. Between 1793 and 1799 the Eastern Regiment was stationed successively at Chichester, Fairlight, Gravesend, Rochester, Hythe and Deal in the southern military district and then at Braintree, Islington, Chelmsford, Norwich itself (briefly in 1797) and finally Ipswich in the eastern district. In 1800 they were moved north to Yorkshire and later were scattered in the manufacturing districts around Stafford, Nottingham, and Derby. After reassembly in Manchester in the following year they were moved back to Chelmsford and then Colchester before being stood down in 1802 at their Yarmouth depot. Between 1793 and 1796 the Western Regiment were successively at Colchester, Danbury, Sudbury, Warley, Hertford, Waltham, Chatham, Malling and Shorncliffe. Records are absent for the next three years but in January 1799 they were again at Colchester.

The existence of the machinery for raising the militia encouraged the government to use it to expand the overall strength of the land forces. In 1796 a supplementary militia was created which tripled the size of the force. In August of that year Norfolk, having returned 17,616 men of an age eligible to serve in the militia plus 1,008 actually serving, was warned to provide a further 1,992 supplementary men. This augmentation was even less popular than the earlier balloting for the original militia. There were numerous riots in protest including an ugly one at Norwich in November when a crowd prevented Townshend from proceeding with a public meeting to implement the Act. A week later he succeeded in completing the formalities, the crowd being intimidated by soldiers parading nearby although elsewhere in the city effigies of Pitt and other politicians were burnt.

The supplementary men were used chiefly in training units and thereafter as a pool of recruits to augment the main militia and the regular forces. However in Norfolk a third regiment of militia was formed with Colonel the Hon Henry Hobart MP in command, and with Thomas Hulton as Lieutenant Colonel. In May 1799 Colonel Hobart died while on leave at Bath. His death had for some time been expected and the attraction of his vacant place, at least in terms of prestige, can be judged from the several applications to replace him received by Lord Townshend. The place went to Thomas Hulton who, as he maintained in a letter written even before the death, had been mainly responsible for bringing the regiment to an efficient condition, but applications came also from John Bedingfield of Ditchingham Hall, Lieutenant Colonel Sir Jacob Astley MP, and Lieutenant Colonel Bulwer, all of which Townshend politely turned down. Bedingfield explained his candidacy as having been made solely on the grounds that he had supposed Hulton might be unable to meet the necessary property qualification. However Hulton had earlier been careful to inform Townshend that he was the designated heir of a richer man, himself a former militia colonel. The now vacant lieutenant colonelcy went to Major Robert Harvey who moved from command of the Norwich Light Horse, a volunteer cavalry troop.

One of Hulton's first tasks was to fill two captaincies vacant through resignations. One of these went to his own brother, Lieutenant George Hulton, previously serving in another Norfolk militia regiment, and the other to young Philip Hamond, son of Anthony Hamond of Westacre. Philip was then only seventeen and still at Eton yet he was to be gazetted captain and command a company. He was escorted from school in September 1799 by his half brother Richard to join the regiment, by then at Worthing, being fitted for his regimentals in London on the way. Perhaps his father's considerable property and influence was the basis for this early promotion but more probably Hulton was influenced equally by kinship for Philip's first cousin Jane Bagge had become Hulton's wife that same year. Still it may have been the former influence that moved Townshend to accept the appointment and recommend it to the War Office. In June 1799 he had received a letter from Colonel Walpole lamenting when making what he seems to have felt was a substandard appointment "that there are no young men of family or superior property in Norfolk who will enter into the service for in my opinion the very existence of the militia does and ought to depend upon the field officers and captains being men of that description ..."

In the last resort family may have been more important than property. When in 1806 Captain Longe applied for a majority in the East Norfolks Townshend supported him, although he could not meet the property qualification, because he had twelve year's service to his credit and, as cousin to Francis Longe of Spixworth Park, he was from "a most ancient and respectable county family". Not all the junior officers in the militia were young. When the adjutant of the West Norfolk Militia, former regular soldier Captain Sir William Gordon, died at Colchester in January 1804 he was aged sixty-six.

In 1799 the militia, previously protected, was thrown open for some weeks as a recruiting ground for the regular forces. In late November the government, at the end of the period allowed for this recruitment of regulars, took steps to effect a temporary reduction in the militia. Norfolk's quota which had been reduced to some 2,250 men, counting old militia and supplementaries together, was to be reduced now by three fifths to just over 900. So far as this had not already been achieved by the loss of those who had joined the regulars it was to be effected by the disbandment of the third regiment and the discharge of any remainder from the two older regiments after such transfers between them as were necessary to equalise numbers. However the Home Secretary warned the lord lieutenant that many of the men might be called up again in the following Spring. It is not clear whether this was done in 1800 but in August 1801, when there was the final invasion scare of the first period of the wars, the supplementary men were being called up once again although the third regiment was never reformed.

Stood down in 1802, the militia was re-embodied in 1803 even before war broke out for the second time and shortly afterwards the supplementary men were also called up. Between 1803 and 1805 recruitment from either type of militia into the regulars was again forbidden. Instead a further force was created, the Army of Reserve, 50,000 men from England, Scotland and Ireland, to be attached to and trained by the regulars and to serve for four years or for the duration specifically as a reservoir of regular recruits not limited to home service. Officers were to come primarily from regulars on half pay. Norfolk's share for this new force was approximately nine hundred men. The ballot was to apply but articled clerks and apprentices under twenty-one and all clergymen were exempt. Parishes had to find substitutes for any Quakers selected. But persons volunteering for any type of militia were to receive a bounty of up to £7 10s 0d equal to half the going rate for hiring a substitute. Notice of assembly for the men recruited for Norfolk was given early in July and the first training began on Chapel Field, Norwich, in early August. Shortly after notice was given that the recruits from the west of the county were to report to the militia depot at East Dereham; those from the east to that at Yarmouth. However in due course training was to be with regular battalions, not with the militia. In the following year the 7th Reserve Battalion, consisting of some 500 men from Norfolk and Suffolk, volunteered to become a regiment of the line.

In 1804 the Army of Reserve and the supplementary militia were merged into a new body, the Permanent Additional Force, and yet further men selected by ballot were to be added as regular army recruitment fodder. By then the nation's reserves of manpower, with numerous men already committed to volunteer units, was severely stretched. Few of the extra men required in 1805 were ever raised. For the remainder of the war the renamed force, as later reorganised into reserve battalions, and the old militia together comprised a pool which became the prime recruiting ground for the regular army. The depleted militia ranks were made up principally by volunteers attracted by bounty, the balloting machinery being used as little as possible and being for some periods suspended altogether. While there were many problems encountered in keeping up numbers in both the regulars and the militia and although the price which had to be paid for substitutes rocketed in times of shortage, a combination of expedients between 1806 and 1815 ensured that sufficient troops were available for overseas expeditions and for the reducing demands of home defence. After 1806 Norfolk was having to find several hundred new men annually.

In March 1803 both Norfolk militia regiments were embodied at their depots and were marched in June to Colchester. There the East Norfolks (and presumably the West Norfolks too) were augmented from a basic establishment of 683 men of all ranks in eight companies to 1057 in ten. In July 1804 both regiments were marched to Coxheath Camp near Maidstone in Kent. In November of 1804 the East Norfolks moved to the south coast, serving first at Winchelsea and then, in the following year, at Hastings. While there new regulations permitted recruiting from militia regiments into the regulars. On this, the first of many occasions of mass volunteering, 156 men from the regiment transferred. There being no means swiftly to make up these numbers and the further needs of the regulars being anticipated, the regiment was allowed, indeed required, to reduce gradually in strength to its establishment of 1803.

In February 1806 they moved back to the Eastern Region, firstly to Chelmsford, then Colchester, then in 1807 to Ipswich, and then, after a spell in 1808/09 at Norman Cross in Northamptonshire guarding prisoners of war, to Woodbridge. During this time they were once again augmented, this time to 914 men but still in only eight companies. They were at Woodbridge for just one month before leaving the region in June 1809 for a new station at Sheerness where they remained for nearly two years. Throughout this time they responded to annual calls for voluntary transfers to the line, sometimes exceeding and sometimes failing to meet a quota, while their strength was made up by new drafts from Norfolk, some balloted and some responding to the blandishments of recruiting parties who worked "by beat of drum". Altogether 634 men left the regiment to join the regulars between November 1804 and December 1811.

In April 1811 they marched from Sheerness to be stationed partly in Margate and partly in Ramsgate. In that year new legislation permitted the use of English and Scottish militia in Ireland (and vice versa), the new Act being read and explained to the regiment by their colonel on 8 July. Out of a total strength that day of 771 all ranks, 678 volunteered to serve in Ireland and on 19 September they were embarked at Ramsgate in three transports. Two of these took eighteen days for the passage to Cork and the third sixty-six, a delay which one must suppose was caused by adverse weather. (The historian of the Norfolk Regiment records that they embarked at Bristol. While the regiment's own records are specific about three ships leaving from Ramsgate the delay to one might have been occasioned by being driven back to Bristol by foul weather.)

Once in Ireland the regiment was stationed firstly at Caher in Tipperary, then at Mallow, and in 1813 at Limerick. During this time there were annual quotas for more volunteers for the line and 150 men were supplied who must have been made up by a greater number of recruits since in April 1813 the strength was 629 or only some fifty less than the force which had embarked at Ramsgate. The regiment embarked again in June 1813, returning to

England at Plymouth in six ships. There they remained, brought up to strength by new Norfolk drafts, for a further year punctuated by a spell on Dartmoor in the winter of 1813/14, once again guarding prisoners of war. Finally in May 1814 they were marched back across the country, taking a full month to reach Yarmouth where the regiment was disembodied.

Less is known of the West Norfolks after 1804. They were on the south coast in 1805 and 1806, first at Dungeness and then at Canterbury. In 1809 they were in Norwich and in 1811 at King's Lynn, moving from there to Woodbridge and Harwich in 1811. In March 1812 they marched north and served variously at Manchester, Stockport, Wakefield, Huddersfield and Sheffield. In April 1813 they marched further north via Berwick to Edinburgh where they remained, stationed at the castle, until returning by sea to Norfolk in July 1814 where they were disembodied. In the following year, when war broke out again after Napoleon's escape from Elba, the newspapers recorded in April that the West Norfolk Militia were raising men once more by beat of drum in Norwich. Their formal embodiment took place in July, and although by then Waterloo had been fought and won they volunteered for service in Ireland where they were stationed until the following April. The East Norfolks were not embodied during the Waterloo coda to the Napoleonic wars or for many years thereafter.

6.   Volunteers to 1801

Having called for volunteers in 1794 the government was anxious to ensure that they were kept firmly under the control of the propertied classes. Volunteer officers were required to have an income from land of not less than fifty pounds per year or to pay rent of not less than one hundred pounds. Sons of persons so qualifying and any person whose military experience was adequate were exempt from the property requirement. Half-pay regular officers were to be preferred to all others, and it seems that there were a considerable number of these in Norfolk. Some care was taken to prevent excessive numbers of higher ranking officers; it was decreed that no volunteer officer should be appointed colonel, while lieutenant colonels were allowed only in units comprising four companies or more. An infantry company - to be not less than sixty nor more than one hundred rank and file - was entitled to a captain, two lieutenants and two ensigns. A corps of two companies was allowed an additional captain in command, while one of three companies was entitled to one major. All officers were required to have some knowledge of the area within which they might be expected to operate. Officers were appointed by the King and at his pleasure; hence they could not resign without his permission. Originally they were to rank as though regular or militia officers notwithstanding how dangerous that might be with command in battle devolving on an inexperienced volunteer who outranked an experienced regular. From 1805 the law was changed and thereafter volunteer officers carried seniority according to their dates of appointment only as against fellow volunteers although there remained problems where a man held both regular and volunteer rank.

Attendance by rank and file at the specified minimum of two days training per week provided exemption from the militia ballot. This was very important in that it provided a means whereby a poor man with a volunteer unit within reach might avoid militia service and the consequent desertion of his family. Two days training might seem very onerous for persons already in full employment but most sessions took place on Saturday afternoons, on Sunday after the main service or, in the summer, on weekday evenings.

Most parts of the county held the meetings to gather subscriptions and register volunteers as advocated by the county defence committee. In the northwest of the county James Coldham of Anmer and Henry Styleman of Snettisham, both magistrates and substantial subscribers to the fund and the latter an ardent Tory, held meetings to gather volunteers for a body of cavalry in their immediate neighbourhood. Following the county lead their object was entirely local "law and order", Coldham writing, "The disaffection of this county prevails to a most alarming degree, and unless something is done to counteract it I fear we shall soon be in a state of confusion." Noting that his fellow magistrate Sir Martin Folkes, MP for Lynn and of equivocal political persuasion, had subscribed, albeit belatedly, £100 to the county fund, Coldham asked him to join and indeed command his and Styleman's unit but already Lord Townshend had recruited Folkes to join the troop being raised in the lord lieutenant's own hundred of Gallow. Folkes actually signed the list of persons to join with Styleman but it would seem that insufficient volunteers were available in that area.

There were difficulties in recruiting the three officers necessary at a minimum for the Gallow troop. Styleman and Coldham, though invited, would not join. Then Lord Townshend found a former regular officer who would act as captain if Folkes would serve under him as lieutenant, but this was too much for Folkes who had told his friends that he was to be captain. He offered instead to withdraw altogether, whereupon Townshend found that the regular officer would be willing to serve under Folkes after all. Eventually the unit, the Norfolk Rangers of 1782 reincarnated, planned initially to be one hundred strong, was formed with Townshend himself as commander and Folkes and two others as the remaining officers, all volunteers finding their own horses but with arms supplied by the Crown. Folkes seems to have brought along many of the men who had offered to join Styleman's troop. Pay for the unit was to be two shillings a day when in training or on service, to be paid out of the county fund which was also to provide uniforms and arms. Half the troops were to be riflemen ["chasseurs"] and the other cavalry, the former to ride behind the latter to the scene of action.

Lynn in past wars had not waited for official blessing for its defence provisions and some local dignitaries were pressing for a town meeting in aid of defence even before the Defence Act passed through Parliament. The first meeting in Lynn took place on 21 April and by June the town had raised its own fund beginning with one hundred pounds from the Corporation itself. Already two companies of volunteer infantry were in being and the town was soon to raise a third. Edward Everard, mayor in 1794 and eldest son of one of the principal merchants, was in command.

The guns on the town's fort, which had been there during the past two wars, proved on inspection to be unserviceable, the wooden gun carriages having rotted. Nevertheless a corps of sea fencibles was recruited whose duty was to repel an attack by sea by manning the guns of any armed ship which happened to be in the harbour at the time. This was not quite as hopeless a plan as it might seem. The Lynn fort was in any case weak being without a parapet, many of the town's ships were armed during the war to repel privateers, and the winding channel below the town made a hostile approach extremely difficult.

The town was already a headquarters for the naval press service and many of its sailors found themselves either pressed or persuaded with bounties into the navy. Lynn was sufficiently satisfied by its subscription fund of over eleven hundred pounds and by its efforts in raising so many soldiers and sailors that the mayor thought it worthwhile to petition the government in 1796 to excuse the town from balloting for the supplementary militia.

Elsewhere in the county initial recruitment was very slow with nothing at all being done in Norwich or Yarmouth. Besides the Norfolk Rangers only three troops of Norfolk yeomanry were accepted in 1794, those centred on East Dereham, on Hingham, (formed by B G Dillingham of Letton who was however "too infirm to be active captain"), and on Loddon. There were just two more the following year (one from the hundreds of Blofield and South Walsham and another from those of Tunstead and Happing) and one double troop in 1796 (Clackclose Hundred with Downham formed by Thomas Hare of Stow Bardolph). All these were specifically for "internal defence"; Townshend wrote that he had great satisfaction in recommending the Blofield & South Walsham troop, "Mr Burroughs [to be captain] being a very able magistrate and having lately by his spirited exertions with that of the neighbouring gentlemen and farmers quelled an attempt of the lower class of people to riot on account of the price of provisions." Apart from the Lynn troops there were no volunteer infantry in Norfolk before 1797: several companies were mooted and one, at Hingham, actually accepted but all appear to have failed and none dating before 1797 appear on the Norfolk returns for 1799.

In theory each unit could choose its own area of operations, whether limited to its parish, its hundred, its county, or the larger area of its local military district ...or indeed anywhere in the country without limit. However the government's permission was required for the formation of any unit and for the commissioning of its officers. In 1794 Townshend was warning some proposers of units that they would not be approved unless they were prepared to serve outside the county not only in the event of actual invasion but also in the event of insurrection. In June a letter from him appeared in the Norfolk papers in which he stated that, it being "expected that the Volunteers may have to march outside the county in the event of riot or insurrection" it was his duty to inform the public "that I have no authority from the Secretary of State to say that there is no such intention on the part of the Government." Even as concealed behind a double negative this was an unpopular decision causing at least one proposal to be aborted.

Acceptance of the Lynn contingent had already been delayed for some weeks during which they were persuaded to increase the radius within which they were prepared to march, the question actually going before Pitt himself. One of Townshend's correspondents observed that an insurrection in another county would be precisely what would most motivate local volunteers to stay at home to guard their own property. But the government's position was that as several midland counties were prepared to march their volunteers to the coast to defend against an invasion it was not unreasonable to expect Norfolk men to march inland if the danger spot lay there. There was also quibbling over the words in the Act which required volunteers to embody and serve under martial law "on the appearance of an invasion". The Lynn commander pointed out that this might just be some landing party from a privateer ashore for loot; his men, mostly small tradesmen, could not afford to leave their businesses for some petty matter of this type.

To worries about riots and insurrections was added fear of invasion in

1797 after the French had failed in an attempt to land in Ireland, even though their diversionary force which had landed at Pembroke had swiftly surrendered. The period of the fleet mutinies in the summer of that year gave rise to particular anxiety although the behaviour of the crews of two mutinous ships temporarily in Yarmouth Roads, who sent delegates ashore to explain their grievances, was eminently reasonable. In June, at the height of the mutinies, the duke of Portland, Home Secretary, circulated lords lieutenant following the issue of a proclamation on suppression of treasonable and rebellious proceedings. They were to communicate with the officers commanding volunteer corps:

> with special instructions to them that they and their respective corps should be aiding and assisting to the civil magistrates in apprehending and securing all persons concerned in the said treasonable and rebellious proceedings their aides and abettors, and to attend to the requisitions which shall be made to them by the magistrates for that purpose.

There were indeed reports of seditious handbills circulating in Norwich in that month although the "patriotic" sentiments of the troops were evident when a gang of regular soldiers prevented the radical speaker Thelwall from holding a public meeting and chased him out of town. While the immediate danger of invasion was removed later in the year by the naval victories at St Vincent and at Camperdown, large numbers of French troops remained encamped on the Channel coast causing a new impetus towards home defence.

Between March 1797 and July 1798 a further nine yeomanry units were raised in Norfolk including the double troop with attached riflemen of the Freebridge Lynn Cavalry formed by banker Joseph Taylor (later the Lynn Legion), the Norwich Light Horse formed by the Harvey family, a cavalry troop at Yarmouth, and at long last the Freebridge & Smithdon troop first mooted in 1794 by Styleman and Coldham. In May 1798 Richard Hamond, having attended the initial subscription meeting, was trying to persuade his father, then away in Bath, to let him join this unit. Its men were to be respectable householders who must be prepared to serve anywhere in Norfolk but principally within their own hundred.

Anthony Hamond was more than doubtful about a unit formed in "his" hundred and in his absence; Mr Coldham should have consulted him first, and Richard was not permitted to join. Some of the original volunteers who were Hamond's tenants had only signed articles subject to his approval, and probably did not join either. The following year on the King's birthday, with his father again away in Bath, Richard wrote that the Lynn Volunteers and Mr Styleman's troop were drawn up in the market place and "cut a very good figure". It is probably significant that when reformed in 1803 the troop was named "Smithdon & Brothercross" while Hamond raised an infantry force in

Freebridge Lynn Hundred with Coldham as his battalion major. Further units of cavalry were proposed for Marshland, for Shropham and Guiltcross hundreds and for Flegg but none came to fruition, the latter because its founder, the Reverend Mr Salmon of Ormesby, was forbidden by the bishop (as were all clergymen) from taking command.

By the same legislation that had raised the supplementary militia in 1796 the government had provided for a cavalry force, "the Provisional Cavalry" by attempting to levy one trooper and one horse for every ten horses kept. Few units of this type were ever raised as the government was prepared to allow corps of yeomanry amounting to three-quarters of the number for which any county stood assessed to be accepted as substitutes. This may as much have been the stimulus for the 1797/8 yeomanry formations in Norfolk as any fear of invasion. In 1798 even Coke of Holkham raised a double yeomanry troop from his tenants after much prodding from his friends who felt he was in danger of losing popular support. Norfolk did raise over 300 men for the Provisional Cavalry by ballot and Lieutenant Colonel Bulwer, back on the half pay list after the demise of his line regiment and eagerly proffering his services to anyone who could find him to a suitable command, was appointed to take charge of this new force.

As a first step he raised a troop of cavalry for South Erpingham and Eynesford hundreds under the provisions of the 1796 Act. Yet by April 1797 he was complaining to Townshend that the men balloted elsewhere were delaying appointing substitutes and as further time was repeatedly allowed them they were hoping they would never be called upon. Notices of muster appeared in the press much later in the year but thereafter there is no mention of the Provisional Cavalry in Norfolk: it was unpopular and was probably stood down once further yeomanry units had been formed. Even Bulwer's own troop converted to a yeomanry unit in May 1799 having in any case always been described as such in returns made of the county's volunteer forces. Bulwer, for the time being confined to this minor command, was ever ready to demonstrate his loyalty and preparedness to do some great deed. Warned by Townshend in 1800 of the possibility of bread riots he reported that his troop was ready at a moments notice and had been issued with twenty rounds of ball cartridge per man, a fearsome approach to dealing with starving men.

General Money received no command at all in this first phase of the war. He was particularly bitter because the command of the Norfolk Provisional Cavalry went to Bulwer rather than to him notwithstanding his superior rank in the army and his much greater experience. Townshend received at least two aggrieved letters from him in which Money emphasised how great an admirer of Townshend he had always been, how good a friend, and yet Townshend had done nothing for him in forty years acquaintanceship. Townshend tried to excuse his choice by pointing out Bulwer's superior property in the county which prompted Money to expound on the evils which had befallen France because the officer corps had been drawn solely from the nobility. Bulwer, wrote Money, might have superior property but nobody could be more zealous or loyal than he while his support of monarchies could be seen from his willingness to risk his life for the French king on that "fatal 10th August" in Paris. Townshend tried to wriggle out of the mess by forwarding Money's letter to the duke of York as commander in chief and asking the government whether his decision might be reversed. However he was told that as Bulwer's appointment had been passed by the King, no change could be made. Townshend must have been relieved at this since Bulwer's wrath might have been even greater had he been relieved of his command almost as soon as he had achieved it!

In 1797 there was only one new infantry unit, the Norwich Loyal Military Association, but this was substantial with some two hundred rank and file. Commanded by John Patteson it seems to have met with opposition and may be seen as a conservative unit as opposed to the strong radical party within the city. At any rate this was an argument used by Patteson in persuading Townshend to allow an establishment of officers greater than normal for fear of offending certain influential persons who had volunteered and whose defection might cause the unit to fail.

With new units forming, others agreed to enlarge the area within which they were prepared to serve. For instance the Tunstead & Happing Cavalry consented in case of imminent invasion to serve anywhere in the county while in the event of actual invasion they were willing to march to any part of the kingdom. The Norfolk Rangers, already engaged to serve anywhere within the county, likewise agreed to serve throughout the kingdom "in the present crisis". The Lynn infantry had started off in 1794 limited to a five mile radius of their town but by 1798 had extended their range to the whole of the eastern district. The new Norwich infantry went one better, specifying "any part of Britain".

A new law, the Defence of the Realm Act, was passed in April 1798 requiring lords lieutenant to obtain returns of the numbers of able-bodied men between the ages of fifteen and sixty resident within their counties, together with particulars of the terms and conditions under which such proportions of the population would be willing to serve. Owners and drivers of horses and cattle, ferrymen, boatmen and labourers were asked to state the terms on which, if called upon, they would be prepared to give their services to the government. Minute directions were given for the classification of the information to be included in the returns which were collected from individual parishes.

A more important provision of the legislation for the volunteer movement was the encouragement of parishes to form armed associations for the protection of persons and property within their local area. The emphasis remained on voluntary service but pay during training or actual service and the all-important exemption from the militia ballot was extended only to members of associations which undertook to serve anywhere within their military district if called upon. On the other hand units would not be refused permission to form however much their area of operations was limited. Membership was to be restricted to respectable householders and others with substantial property and it is clear from surviving correspondence that this restriction operated to slow recruitment and in some cases to cause proposed units to be abandoned.

Before August 1798 armed associations of infantry had been formed at Wells, North Walsham, Yarmouth (2 companies), Thetford, Diss and Old Buckenham and in at least seven Norwich parishes plus an artillery unit to man the Cromer battery. In addition sea fencibles were recruited at Yarmouth In April 1798 the *Norfolk Chronicle* recorded that the sea fencibles of Gorleston had paraded in the town and then "proceeded to the battery on Gorleston Cliff where they exercised the 24 and 32 pounders in the most able and spirited manner". It is unclear who, if anyone, was manning the batteries along the Yarmouth seafront before 1798; perhaps reliance was being placed on such seamen as might have been in the harbour at the time of an emergency. There was a constant demand for sergeants from the regulars to drill units of every type. Not all the Norwich parish proposals were approved by Townshend; three at least were refused with that from the parish of St Johns Maddermarket turned down as composed of persons of "very doubtful loyalty". Even the so-called Norwich Loyal Military Association was purged in 1800 of certain men whose loyalty was suspected. Nor did all the associations last. The Thetford company and two of the Norwich parish associations had failed by 1800.

Despite this surge of activity returns for the county show that the volunteer units in existence in the autumn of 1798 (excluding sea fencibles) had less than three thousand men in their ranks taking yeomanry and infantry together. Many of these were severely limited in their volunteered range of service. While the yeomanry troops formed in 1797 or before were without exception prepared to serve throughout the county and in most cases well beyond, those formed in 1798, whether cavalry or infantry, especially the new armed associations, were often substantially more limited. For example the Yarmouth contingents and those of the Norwich parishes would serve only within their town and its immediate neighbourhood while the Diss infantry would not go outside their home hundred. As these restrictions meant that no Government pay or allowances could be received there was a new wave of local subscriptions to provide funds, the central county fund being exhausted. A summary of 1800 shows that the Norfolk volunteer corps (some of more than one company or troop) would serve:

In any part of England	5
Within the Eastern Military District	9
Within 20 miles radius of home base	8
Limited to their own town	4
Within City of Norwich only	6

Whatever the government's hope it is clear that from Norfolk at least it could not draw any form of homogenous force that could be manoeuvred as a whole. And even without considering limitations on areas of service Norfolk's success in raising volunteers fell well behind that of some of the more threatened counties in the south. In 1798, when Norfolk still had less than three thousand volunteers under arms, the Isle of Wight had over six thousand and Devon nearly nine thousand. Yet there were prospects of an enemy landing until shortly before the first phase of the wars ended. As late as August 1801 the Norwich parish volunteers were paraded in the market place to hear read a letter from Townshend warning them to prepare for an imminent invasion.

1. Two members of the Norwich Rifle Corps, raised and commanded by Richard Mackenzie Bacon, a Norfolk musician and journalist who subsequently edited the *Norwich Mercury*. The riflemen considered themselves the elite amongst the Norwich units and took pride in receiving no government funds for their equipment and uniforms.

2. Colonel John Harvey, commandant of the Norwich Light Horse originally raised by his brother Robert. This impressive portrait of Harvey and his horse by the fashionable artist John Opie (1761–1807) was presented to the City by his brother officers in 1803 and now forms part of the Norwich collection of mayoral portraits.

3. Colonel John Patteson who raised and commanded the Norwich Battalion of Volunteer Infantry and later commanded the 2nd Eastern Battalion of Norfolk Local Militia. A rich woolmerchant and brewer, he was prominent in local politics and served as MP for the City from 1806 to 1812. His massive house in Surrey Street still stands but he became impoverished in his last years after financial failure. This picture by Sir William Beechey (1753–1839), like that of Harvey, forms part of the Norwich collection of mayoral portraits.

4A. Shooting prize badge from the Norwich Volunteer Battalion. The musketeer depicted appears to be wearing a uniform more appropriate for hunting than soldiering at that time.

4. Badge of a unit entitled the Diss Light Infantry. Presumably this was identical to the body otherwise known as the Diss Volunteer Infantry and represents the only known indication that it may have trained and manoeuvred at the faster pace of light infantry skirmishers.

5. Jacket and helmet of a private in the East Norfolk Militia.

6. West Norfolk militia private *c*.1808

7. West Norfolk militia drummer c. 1800, but before the abolition of the queue or pigtail.

8. The title to one version of this engraving of Cromer is "*Sea fencibles drilling on the Marrams. The Lord Suffield of the day in command*". However it seems unlikely that sea fencibles, mainly fishermen to be employed in boats or as artillerymen, would be dressed in the manner of those drilling with such apparent precision.

7.   Volunteers in 1803 – The Rush to Arms

Following the announcement of peace negotiations in October 1801 and a peace treaty in the following spring most volunteer units disbanded. Despite early evidence suggesting that it should have been seen as no more than a temporary truce the peace was widely welcomed in Norfolk. In May of 1802 a meeting of the "late" Holkham Yeomanry Cavalry resolved to dine annually in future years on 6th May, the birthday of their commander Thomas Coke. While nationally a number of volunteer units were anxious to continue in existence and lobbied to do so, the government was unwilling to permit this unless they were prepared to go without financial support. Nevertheless an Act was passed in June 1802 allowing the King to accept the services of yeomanry and volunteer infantry and artillery units on such terms and conditions as he might see fit – which basically meant no pay or allowances – and in October eleven of the Norfolk yeomanry units of the previous war were accepted under this new legislation.

In March a portrait of John Harvey, commander of the Norwich Light Horse, wearing his regimental uniform, was placed in St Andrews Hall with the city's collection of mayoral portraits. But even before the Holkham veterans could hold their first annual dinner the militia were again being embodied and soon after war was once again declared. Although the regular army had not been run down anywhere near as far as at the end of earlier wars, with an immediate threat of a French invasion there was an urgent need to recruit it further and an equally pressing need to recreate a home defence force. The initial result was chaos, verging on panic. The supplementary militia were called up in May and in June a new recruitment Act provided for forty thousand additional seamen. This was closely followed by the Act creating the Army of Reserve (see Chapter 5).

The next month saw the "General Defence", or "Levy en masse Act". This provided for a two-pronged approach to the threat of invasion. Firstly there were plans for what was called "driving the country", a mass evacuation of non-combatants and livestock from the coastal areas in which an invasion had occurred. Secondly able bodied men in every parish of the country were to be formed into local units, issued with arms, and taught how to use them. Their job would be to stay behind and fight as auxiliaries to the regular troops and militia or to act as guides or pioneers. Selection was to be by ballot and service to be under officers from the parish but this near approach to universal conscription was to be avoided if possible. So it was decreed that compulsory enrolment for any county would be suspended in the event that the number of volunteers amounted to three-quarters of the whole number that the Act otherwise required to be selected by ballot.

In early June ministers had been saying in Parliament that it was not the intention to raise volunteer units on the scale that had been achieved in the war immediately preceding but they also announced quite generous allowances for those volunteer units which had by then been accepted provided they undertook fairly extensive training. By August in consequence of the General Defence Act they had on their hands the largest mass volunteering for armed service that the country had ever seen. Although some units were prepared to be self supporting financially and some were prepared to serve anywhere in the kingdom at least in the event of actual invasion, others had more restrictive aims. It was decided that, as with the armed associations of the previous part of the war, volunteer corps would qualify for pay during training and actual service and for exemption from the militia ballot only if they agreed to serve at any point within their local military district. Despite this restriction and a sharp cut in the allowances to be paid to those volunteers accepted after July, soon so many had come forward that the government was attempting to limit the total enrolled in a given area to six times its militia requirement or roughly three hundred thousand for the country overall.

Despite the overlay of panic the entire approach to the possibility of invasion was considerably more businesslike than it had been in the previous decade. The lords lieutenant were instructed to divide their counties into subsidiary military districts or divisions each in charge of one or more deputy lieutenants. These latter were in turn to appoint inspectors to administer the several hundreds which fell within each district, while the inspectors were to seek out and appoint persons, each to take responsibility as superintendent of a parish. All these posts were to be voluntary and were to be given only to persons of local standing and influence, that is to say in practice to the gentry and clergy. Liaison with the regular forces and control over the whole system of command was carried out in Norfolk by weekly meetings in Norwich of the senior deputy lieutenants, attended also by senior army officers and the bishop of Norwich. Questions considered ranged from the issue of the evacuation plans and the placing of signal stations, through the recruitment of special constables, down to such minor detail as the accumulation of ammunition for privately owned fowling pieces.

As in 1798 there were orders for collection of statistics on the resources available in each parish. Whereas the returns for 1798 do not appear to have survived, summaries of those for 1803 were seen by Mason who published a summary in his 1886 *History of Norfolk*. From there it is possible to glean the numbers of oxen, cows, sheep, pigs, riding horses, draught horses, wagons and carts for each division as well as extensive information on grain and other food stocks. All this had been collated and passed on to Whitehall though it is hard to see what use could have been made of it there. Mason also provides a few manpower statistics but these relate only to a few of Norfolk's hundreds and perhaps may never have been completed for the whole county.

A system of coastal signal stations was to be established in accordance with plans issued by the Navy Office; Sandringham and Docking were to be two of the sites. These would be supplemented by a chain of coastal warning beacons much on the lines of those set up in Elizabethan times. Folkes and Coldham were the deputy lieutenants responsible for the erection of these beacons on the coast of northwestern Norfolk. However communications were still far from perfect. Edward Pratt of Ryston wrote worriedly in August to Anthony Hamond, a fellow deputy lieutenant, that he had heard that a beacon was to be placed at Shouldham or Fincham but needed military advice as to where it should be sited since he presumed it had to communicate with others. He continued, "I think our lord lieutenant quite superannuated for I can get no answer from him. My orders were that a meeting was to be fix'd for that purpose but I have heard nothing more." He went on to ask Hamond to get a professional opinion from Captain Shields, the commander of the Lynn sea fencibles.

When enemy forces were sighted offshore warning signals were to be made by the troops watching the coast and further, more urgent signals were to follow, with beacons lighted if a landing was effected or in course. Should such occur then red flags were to be flown from church towers and the church bells rung, while if the landing was within thirty miles of any parish local evacuation and mobilisation was to take place for which the plans should have been laid well in advance. Flagposts were also set up at three of the principal country houses of the county, Raynham, Holkham and Houghton. Such local carriages and wagons as had not already been committed to military use would be used to move the elderly, the infirm and young families to safer areas, with youngsters and the remaining female population accompanying them on foot. Baggage was to be strictly limited but all were to take a blanket and some rations. Those having to ride were to be issued in advance with tickets specifying in whose wagon they were to be accommodated and where they were to assemble to be picked up.

While all military, pioneer and guide volunteers were to report to their units, some men were to have been detailed to drive off (or if necessary kill or hamstring) stock with priority given to horses and cattle which might be of immediate use to an invading force either as cavalry mounts or draught animals. Flocks of sheep and other animals which might feed an invader were to follow if time permitted. Certain wagons were to be handed over to the military while any residual wheeled vehicles were to have their wheels or axles smashed. The evacuation was to avoid major roads which must be kept clear so that troops could be rushed forward to combat the enemy The general direction of the civil retreat was to be westward to beyond Wisbech, with Norwich, Yarmouth and Lynn being left well stocked with provisions for the defending forces. The likely confusion may well be imagined. Happily the practicality of all this was never put to the test and later in the year much of this feature of the invasion plans was quietly dropped.

An eloquent letter of early August to the deputy lieutenants from the Reverend Mr Salmon of Ormesby, now the inspector of the district of Flegg, explained that with some difficulty he had persuaded the inhabitants of his area of the necessity of evacuation in the face of invasion but had totally failed to get them to volunteer to fight. While he deplored their lack of spirit, he admitted that they had a point. How could they, unformed and virtually unarmed, be expected to resist an organised invader? There were no regular troops defending the area and only a single militia regiment in Yarmouth without even a field piece. Why could not a defensive redoubt be set up on Acle heights armed with cannon? Then at least it would be clear that there was some basis for an area defence. At much the same time the *Norfolk Chronicle* reported that Salmon had published "a very spirited address" to the inhabitants of Flegg in which he had said that he had it "on good authority" that 60,000 men were assembled in Holland for invasion. Despite this the *Norfolk Chronicle* seems to have felt that people were not alarmed enough. The editor, in the edition for 23 July, considered that ministers were too relaxed about invasion. The British press must save the country by sounding the alarm:

> We entertain confident hopes that in a few weeks the greatest part of the male population of the country will be voluntarily in arms. .... Let not the measures taken for the defence of everything that is dear to us be stigmatised as acts of oppression; nor our generals libelled and sneered at; and we may expect not only unanimity but a love of military fame and glory to prevail even in this city.

In early July 1803, before the government made its cry for volunteers or had introduced the Bill for a levy-en-masse, General Money had met the lieutenancy of the county – the lord lieutenant and deputy lieutenants assembled – and addressed them on the urgent need to prepare for an invasion. It would seem that they were unresponsive, pleading that forming armed associations without Parliamentary authority might be illegal. Later in the month, the government having brought forward its new Bill, he published an address which he had, he said, written before the meeting. Simultaneously he published another addressed to the farmers of the county and anyone else who could bear arms. In these he explained why he thought Norfolk, although no target for a main French invasion, might all too likely be the scene of a diversionary raid aimed at capturing Norwich and drawing forces away from the defence of London and the south. His remedy was to urge the formation of armed associations in every village and town.

Although he had information (like many English gentlemen he had seized the opportunity of the peace to make a visit to Paris) that the French had accurate knowledge of the Yarmouth approaches, he now believed that if a landing was effected it would probably be at Pakefield or Southwold Bay in north Suffolk aimed at seizing first Lowestoft and Lothing, and that this would be impossible to prevent. But if then the invaders marched on Norwich – and there were very few routes by which they could – and could not without cannon be stopped at Beccles Dam, then they should not be opposed directly but the country should rise on their flanks and in their rear, harassing them from all sides but never attempting to fight in the open.

He believed neither their cannon nor their cavalry could operate effectively in the enclosed countryside of east Norfolk. However by lining hedges with sharpshooters who retired once attacked in force, by picking off foraging parties and any stragglers, and by preventing any enemy transport from using the roads without escorts drawn from their main body, the French who arrived at Norwich might be forced into an untenable position yet unable to retreat by the way they had come. If then British irregular troops could seize Acle, break the causeway and destroy the bridge while taking away all craft on the Bure, the French might not be able to go forward either. Money completed this optimistic scenario with a possible French capitulation before Acle. He did not seem very worried that the French might for a while occupy Norwich; one has the impression that he thought it would be a salutary event for the citizens of the city.

In this pamphlet Money argued against using raw troops in the open against veterans and cannon:

> ...I am perfectly of [the] opinion, that your Militia will at the first onset be unequal to a contest with veteran troops, if such the army of France be composed. I know what raw soldiers are, in any country; when put in the situation of troops of the line, they are not to be depended upon, a single cannon shot will sometimes send them to the right about; there are two descriptions of troops that are more subject to panic than any other, viz. troops who have never been in action, and men accustomed to be beaten. It has been my lot to have been in three armies that have been beaten, that at Saratoga, that in Brabant, where we had 40,000 men and not a man could be made to halt, and form in a retreat of 30 miles, also in the army under Dumouriez in Champagne, and nothing but the confidence they received from the junction of 30,000 men under Kellerman, prevented them from disbanding altogether.

He recalled the British campaign in America where Burgoyne's army, "the finest army in the world", unable to forage for fear of being cut off and unable to use their laboriously hauled cannon in wooded country, laid down their arms at Saratoga to "an undisciplined rabble", the New York and New England militias who knew the country, were experienced in woodcraft and trained to fire from behind trees. Whether his equation of twenty miles of Norfolk road and farmland to be traversed by the French on their route to Norwich with the three hundred miles south from Montreal through lake and forest country travelled by Burgoyne was reasonable must be open to doubt, but the tactics he proposed could have been superior to the formal defence by massed infantry and cavalry in open field or heathland that the more conventional soldiers would have preferred.

His address to the farmers is stirring stuff indeed. He urges them either to wake up now, or do so one night when they find a French patrol at their door, their wives and daughters raped, their barns fired, their horses and cattle driven off, and they themselves forced at bayonet point to drive transport for the enemy. "The sort of war we have to fight is firing from hedge row to hedge

45

row, and way lay the enemy in every direction they are likely to pass." "One thousand good marksmen are more than a match for two thousand highly dressed regiments which were never trained to act as irregulars." He urged that the government policy of driving the country -removing cattle and horses from the coastal area- was totally impracticable; it was a pity the policy did not cover frogs as well as cattle "for the French will eat either". It was necessary to defend the country, not empty it.

He quoted from Windham in Parliament a few weeks earlier saying that what was needed was not uniforms or foppery. A riband or an armband would be enough. There need be no drums or fifes, no marching in rank and file, but firing at a mark, technique in cleaning arms, and training in lining hedges, firing from behind trees, retiring on call and in resuming station. Money elaborated on this advising complete silence in manoeuvre, oak leaves in hats for recognition and a sportsman's whistle for a signal. Boys of sixteen, useless as infantry of the line, would do excellently in irregular tactics being more daring than their elders. All should practise marksmanship and obtain ball cartridge for their fowling pieces. "No drilling is required; no facing to the right; nor facing to the left, is necessary; if a man has sense enough to know his right hand from his left, he has sense enough to know a Frenchman when he sees him, and to kill him when he can." And he quoted Sir Andrew Agnew at Culloden to his men, "There are your enemies, if you do na kill them, by God they will kill you."

Townshend, also with American experience, would certainly have been sympathetic, and later asserted that those troops formed and armed as riflemen or sharpshooters would prove the most effective should invasion occur. At the end of July he was proposing to the government that the county's volunteer forces should be divided into two, the western half being commanded by Bulwer and the eastern by Money, "a very active, zealous officer and has seen a great deal of service." In the event this plan was not adopted but at the end of the year Money was placed in charge of the Eastern Norfolk Cavalry, about 350 officers and men, (Bulwer having a similar unit based in central Norfolk). These he promptly began to augment by recruiting sharpshooters and pioneers, saying that without foot soldiers in support and pioneers to break gaps in hedges his cavalry were as useless in close country as he had earlier considered the French cavalry to be. However he does not seem to have been able to persuade his horse soldiers to train to fight dismounted and, for all his and Townshend's enthusiasm for irregular tactics, most of the Norfolk infantry proceeded to organise themselves as conventional troops of the line.

In April Lord Townshend had issued an invitation for infantry volunteers although there was little immediate response except that the Norwich Loyal Military Association was re-established on May 3 with some 300 men agreeing to serve in what became the Norwich Battalion of infantry commanded, as in the previous period of the war, by John Patteson. Then on 6 August the lieutenancy issued a ringing patriotic proclamation calling for enough volunteers to avoid the compulsory provisions of the General Defence Act. The response was immediate and overwhelming. Within the month meetings had been held in all the principal towns and in many country districts, volunteers enrolled, officers chosen, and subscriptions raised to fund arms and equipment. Lynn had raised three hundred men by 10 August and two weeks later had six hundred volunteers as well as four hundred sea fencibles. Sea fencibles were also recruited at Yarmouth, Cromer, and Wells, some 250 at the latter town alone.

At a meeting in Norwich midway through the month, after a long and bombastic speech by Lieutenant Colonel Robert Harvey, reported at length in the *Norfolk Chronicle*, over one thousand men had volunteered for a new Norwich regiment, while the city's subscription fund had reached three thousand pounds and Major Richard Bacon was raising a company of riflemen. Each week the newspaper had further reports of numerous companies being recruited up and down the county. By the end of August six thousand men had volunteered throughout Norfolk out of a total of just over seven thousand needed to avert local balloting and the numbers were still rising. In early October officers appointed to twenty-eight different Norfolk units were referred to in just one edition of the Gazette. By the end of November there were in existence forty infantry units, most of just a single company but some as in Norwich and other towns of more, while further cavalry troops had been formed or reformed to bring the total to twenty-two.

No unit proposed failed to achieve its initial targets and there was less jealousy over recruiting areas than there had been earlier. The Cromer artillery company, having reformed, threatened to resign en masse when sea fencibles were also recruited in the town, but this was due to some misunderstanding of their proposed roles and the problem was swiftly sorted out. Less care was taken by the lieutenancy to examine the loyalty and motives of those volunteering than had been the case five years earlier. No unit was refused and approvals went through without much scrutiny. Partly this was because the government was far less concerned about insurrection; partly because the overwhelming response was quite beyond the resources for review and scrutiny available to the Home Office, to which responsibility for volunteers had been transferred.

By September, although there was a serious shortage of arms, and few of the men were yet in uniform, many units were in training. So concerned was the government at the scale (and hence expense) of the recruitment response yet so unhappy to damp the new-found enthusiasm that units were permitted to take on supernumeraries although these could not be paid during training. Meanwhile Lord Townshend was begging for two thousand stand of arms to be sent down to the county and ordering a census of arms of any sort already held privately. At Lynn the Lynn & Freebridge Yeomanry Cavalry under Major Taylor had paraded on a Sunday at the beginning of September and marched to South Lynn to attend a church service together with the infantry company being raised in that parish. The Reverend Mr Coulcher wrote to

Anthony Hamond from Wisbech that his curate at Westacre had told him, "...you were all soldiers in your parishes where complete unanimity prevailed." At Wisbech there were three hundred infantry in the neighbourhood, "...nothing but volunteers of both sorts." Even quite tiny communities were organising their own companies. For instance the *Norfolk Chronicle* recorded on September 24 that:

> On Friday last the Barton Bendish Loyal Volunteers...had a field day; after the company, which consists of 60 privates, had gone through their exercise, they retired under a covered way to a plentiful provision of roast beef, plumb puddings and ale; when the utmost harmony prevailed, several loyal toasts and songs were sung, and a subscription entered into when £75 was immediately subscribed by the farmers of the above parish.

No doubt such a scene was being repeated through much of the county. But not all of the county. For plotting the bases of the units raised shows that most of Norfolk's numerous parishes do not feature and some hundreds raised no cavalry at all (See Map 4). Partly this may be explained because volunteers from parishes close to towns chose to join town units, and where one hundred (Freebridge Lynn) raised the majority of an infantry battalion, a muster list shows that its three companies drew their men from twenty-seven different parishes within the hundred. Nevertheless it is noticeable that quite large areas can have contributed nobody. For instance there was no cavalry unit in fifteen out of thirty-two hundreds, and in ten hundreds no infantry unit in even one parish. The hundreds of Wayland, Depwade, Henstead, Humbleyard and East and West Flegg had no unit of either kind. Most towns had at least one company of infantry but not Attleborough or Wymondham.

Linda Colley suggests that East Anglia's relatively poor performance was because "the rural hinterland...was simply too sparsely populated, too in-sulated, too complacent within itself to care much about the nation beyond its borders". But this does not really match the pattern of recruitment in Norfolk where volunteers were numerous in some rural areas while others produced none. The village of North Elmham was the only parish in Launditch Hundred to produce any volunteers at all but mustered nearly one hundred on its own. It would seem that the creation of a volunteer unit depended very much on the influence, enthusiasm and energy and perhaps also the political leanings of one or more of the principal inhabitants or landlords. Parts of Norfolk, and especially the larger towns, managed to amass the target total of six times the county militia without any call upon the rest.

By the end of November 1803 the number of volunteers was large enough to satisfy the General Defence Act but the new units were in most cases scarcely useful as military formations. They were first inspected by a professional soldier, in November and December at a time when many still had neither uniforms nor satisfactory arms. At this early stage the inspector,

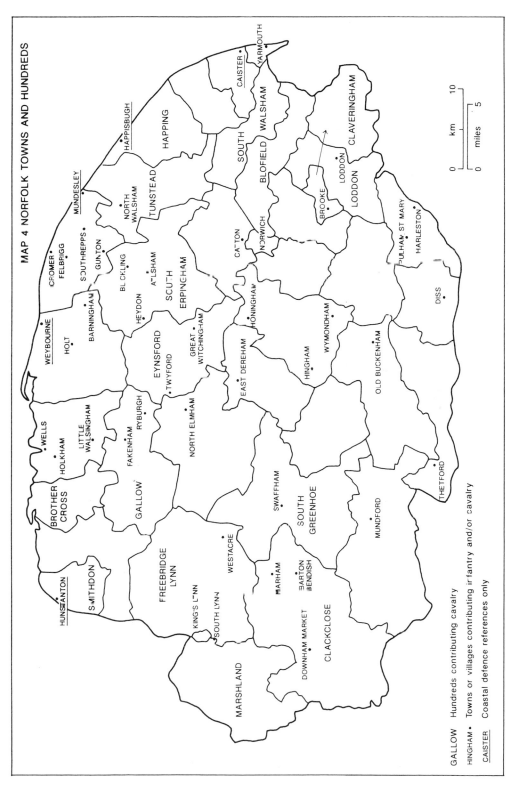

MAP 4 NORFOLK TOWNS AND HUNDREDS

GALLOW   Hundreds contributing cavalry

HINGHAM• Towns or villages contributing infantry and/or cavalry

CAISTER   Coastal defence references only

49

Lieutenant Colonel Metzner, formerly of the Oxfordshire Fencible Cavalry and now called back from half pay, was invariably kind in his assessments. Even what must have been a shocking sight for a regular soldier drew no worse comment than "a fine body of men, but as yet undisciplined".

Sometimes officers were "as yet uninstructed" but usually they were "very attentive". Arms, if any, were frequently Prussian or "mixed British and foreign" and uniforms occasionally "in course of making". The worst comment was usually a terse "recently raised" or "new unit". Clearly there was much to be done but every hope that it would be.

8.   The Volunteers at their Zenith

One method was contrived which gave the more advanced units an opportunity to train together and indeed to perform a potentially useful service. At the end of October 1803 the Yarmouth garrison was if anything less than it had been when Salmon complained of its inadequacy in August, with just some elements of the Shropshire Militia in the town. From Newmarket a sporting friend of Anthony Hamond wrote that month, "We dare not put too much into the salting trough fearing Bonaparte will visit us from your unguarded coast on his way to the metropolis." A meeting of deputy lieutenants complained that not enough was being done and made their feelings known via the newspapers. More arms and some mobile artillery were required. Lord Townshend wrote to London complaining that although other areas might be more at risk Norfolk too was a likely invasion target and Yarmouth a port and naval base of too great an importance to neglect. Could not some more troops be spared? Simultaneously he circulated the new volunteer units asking which would agree to be embodied to garrison Yarmouth for a week in turn.

There is no report of any refusals and the first in what became a regular rota during the ensuing year were the Norwich Volunteer Infantry under Patteson, the Fakenham company of Loyal Volunteers under Captain Mallet Case, and the Norfolk Rangers, Colonel Lord Townshend himself (Field Marshall on the retired list, veteran of Dettingden in 1743, Culloden in 1746 and Quebec in 1759, and now aged 82) riding at their head. Other units followed, some serving for more than a week, their movements reported obsequiously in the newspapers from which one learns that they had behaved impeccably and were "much improved" by this service. No doubt they were, but one trembles to think what they must have been like before!

Although the first tide of enthusiasm for the volunteers was perhaps slackening by the winter they remained popular in many quarters. The second Dereham cavalry troop, returning home from Yarmouth service in early January 1804 were "elegantly" entertained at Caister by a Mr Brandford who provided a "sumptuous cold collation" (although perhaps hot soup would have been better appreciated). Others with thoughts for the comfort of the troops were the ladies of Lynn who were subscribing to sew undergarments for the Lynn battalion. Cut out cloth, using four yards of flannel serge, was available from a local tailor at five shillings a set comprising a sleeved waistcoat and pair of drawers to be made up at home. Eight hundred sets had been subscribed for by January.

In February 1804 an Act was passed to consolidate earlier legislation governing volunteer forces. In this the right of any ranker volunteer to resign, which had previously been of doubtful legality, was confirmed. In addition the position regarding exemption from the militia ballot was regularised. To refer to exemption is in fact a simplification of the position, since the names of all volunteers had to be amongst those balloted and they were only exempt from service if they could produce a certificate of having attended a required minimum of training. The new Act fixed this minimum at twenty-four days full time training each year (or equivalent) and made this figure equally applicable for exemption from the militia and from the Army of Reserve.

Before the end of 1803 lords lieutenant had been instructed to reorganise their cavalry into regiments and their infantry into battalions. Townshend had begun the task with enthusiasm, starting with the cavalry, although difficulties soon became apparent. Two regiments, Midland and Eastern commanded by Bulwer and Money, were created by incorporating local troops without much trouble although Bulwer made some difficulty. He wished to bring into his cavalry regiment (or at least exclude from any larger infantry unit) the Heydon Volunteer Infantry company of which he was also commander, explaining that he had raised the unit on the promise that they would not be separated from their neighbours in the Erpingham & Eynesford Yeomanry Cavalry. He could not see why his regiment should not have some foot soldiers attached as did Townshend's own Norfolk Rangers or, for that matter, the Lynn Legion which had cavalry, riflemen and even some artillery.

Bulwer's protest, repeated several times, was ultimately in vain and yet logic was on his side for, as already related, shortly after Money had assumed his command he raised companies of sharpshooters and pioneers to be attached to his formation. However the main organisational problem at this stage was with the First Norfolk Cavalry of which Townshend himself was to be commander. This was to include the Norfolk Rangers, complete with its riflemen, the mixed Lynn Legion under Joseph Taylor, and the pure cavalry units from Holkham, Marshland, and Smithdon & Brothercross. This unit never did effectively combine. The Lynn contingent simply refused to join, declining even to send returns of strength via Townshend's adjutant, while the small Marshland troop was just too far away.

It was not only the senior officers who had feelings to be considered. Some idea of the touchiness of more junior officers can be gained from the following letter dated 17 January 1804 from Lord Townshend to Sir Martin Folkes once again one of his captains in the Rangers:

> I have received an intimation of your feelings upon the circumstance of the regimental arrangement of our Corps rendering you liable in the event of its being called into service to be under the command of an officer your inferior in the rank of society. Believe me nothing can be more repugnant to my disposition than to propose any arrangement in which you might be concerned that had a tendency to wound your feelings: the measure of regimenting the Corps was directed by Government, and in the appointment of officers which I proposed I was governed by a strict impartiality and a just defference [sic] to property.
>
> I was not unmindful of your claim to military promotion, and used my

best endeavours to advance it, but the Government (influenced by impartiality) was not disposed to deviate from established rules.

I should feel much distressed at your retiring from the Corps from the motives aforenamed and felt desirous to do every thing in my power consistent with the good of the Corps and of the service that can dispel such a sentiment from your mind. Upon considering the circumstances which you intimate of the flanks of the Regiment in the event of the Chasseurs being detached from them I am led to think that it would be an eligible arrangement if we were to form one troop entirely of riflemen and leave the other as light dragoons, in such an arrangement I beg to be informed if it would be agreeable to you to command the troop of chasseurs, which would generally act upon detached service and consequently not expose you to be under that command which you disapprove.

Sir Martin must have been won over by this dubious rearrangement of a tactical unit to salve private feelings for a year later Townshend endorsed his promotion to major. At that time William Hoste of Barwick, now commanding the Smithdon & Brothercross troop, wrote to him saying that had anyone else been appointed over him he, Hoste, would have resigned, and expressing some contempt for volunteer rank now that the Gazette was full of militia and volunteer officers who would never have been considered gentlemen. Hoste had spent seven years in the Royal Horse Guards (Blues), a unit favoured by young Norfolk gentlemen which, though less grand and expensive than the Life Guards, was grand enough to make later yeomanry service seem somewhat plebeian. Philip Hamond, whose early start in the militia has already been referred to, also spent time in the Blues, as did Edmund Rolfe from Heacham who later became a captain in Coke's Holkham troop. In early 1804 the Yarmouth troop of cavalry split over some question of precedence and approximately half the troop resigned, leaving the commander to recruit it back to strength in the ensuing months.

If the cavalry had its problems, those arising from Townshend's efforts to produce eleven infantry battalions were worse. With the exception of Lynn and Yarmouth, each of which had enough men to form one battalion on its own, the main problem was linking together under one command companies which were often miles apart so that in practice they could seldom or never train as one battalion unit. A further difficulty was the several different types of company which had been formed, some nominated light infantry, some riflemen, some sharpshooters and some simply infantry. The first three types would have practised different modes of drill and manoeuvre from the others and aspired to have different weapons. Townshend and Money would have preferred all to be irregulars but the government instructions were to form conventional line battalions. It might have been acceptable to attach one company of light infantry or the like to each infantry battalion but what was

Townshend to do with the six companies of the Blickling & Gunton Riflemen, formed and commanded by his rival and eventual successor as lord lieutenant, Colonel Harbord, which was by far the largest unit north of Norwich? In fact he gave up. The Third Norfolk Battalion, which was to include both the Blickling and Heydon units was never formed.

Norwich was another special case. Harvey's Norwich Regiment, with ten companies, was easily large enough on its own to form a battalion but there were also Patteson's Norwich Battalion of infantry which was the senior formation yet smaller than acceptable battalion size and the Norwich Riflemen under Richard Bacon whose men preferred to resign rather than merge with Patteson's unit as was proposed. Just outside Norwich were the Loyal Catton Sharpshooters under Jeremiah Ives who were never merged, not even with the Fifth Battalion, a unit already hopelessly spread between Aylsham, North Elmham, East Dereham and Hingham. Major George Walpole had commanded the Aylsham company but resigned after protest when the unit was to be placed in the Fifth Battalion. He had been briefly a local Major General while serving in Jamaica and could not face being placed under some officer who would formerly have been his junior. The companies at Honingham, Barningham and Great Witchingham were never brigaded at all, and that at South Lynn, logically best brigaded with the main Lynn battalion, was placed in Townshend's plans together with the battalion of Freebridge Lynn hundred and, in all probability due to local jealousies, had no relationship in practice with either.

Whereas in the 1790s Anthony Hamond of Westacre had declined to have anything to do with the volunteer forces, in 1803 he formed two companies based mainly on his own estates. The majority of his officers certainly seem to qualify as gentlemen. His two captains were Henry Elsden from a well known Lynn merchant family, and John Turner Hales, nephew of Sir Martin Folkes. Richard Hamond, his eldest son, was one of the three lieutenants and a younger son, Robert, a Cambridge undergraduate, was an ensign. In the previous summer Richard had been drawn in the militia ballot at Westacre and it had been necessary to buy a substitute.

Another lieutenant was the Honourable Prescott Blencowe, a relation by marriage of the prosperous Everard merchant family at Lynn which supplied also the colonel of the Lynn battalion, while James Coldham, son of Mr Coldham of Anmer, fellow magistrate of Folkes and Hamond, was an ensign. Only the connections of Lieutenant John Brett and Ensign Henry Standford have not been traced. A friend writing from Bath in January 1804 had heard that, "the whole county is almost in arms, Bravo!" and a month later wrote, "I hear ...that the Westacre Volunteers make a most respectable appearance and that the Major has a very military look indeed ... I wish I could take a peep at them." Later Hamond became colonel of the Eleventh Battalion after the incorporation of Henry Styleman's Smithdon company, a promotion which acknowledged his social precedence in west central Norfolk, while Coldham senior became the battalion major.

From December 1803 onwards and particularly in the following spring the papers report frequent training exercises including some quite realistic mock battles, some in conjunction with regulars and militia, in such areas as Bramerton Common, the denes at Yarmouth, and on the heathlands to the east of Lynn. In one exciting exercise at Cromer sea fencibles and sailors acted as invading forces, landing on the beach and storming the town and a fort which was defended by volunteer infantry and the corps of Cromer Battery Volunteers. The Norwich units are reported on several occasions as having taken part in joint exercises with the 24th Foot which then formed the Norwich regular garrison. Whatever the inspecting officers thought (to judge by the newspapers they were invariably highly pleased) much training must have been required before the Norwich troops (all the infantry units) could perform as they are reported to have done at Hellesdon in early May 1804 when they:

> marched in review order, in ordinary and quick time, performed the fourth and fifth manoeuvres, advanced by alternate companies, changed position by echelon movement, retired by wings and advanced in line with charged bayonets. During these manoeuvres the brigade fired by platoons, grand divisions and wings and also two volleys of the whole line.

Yet this was just the sort of parade ground manoeuvre that Money would have condemned as useless because incapable of being performed successfully by unbloodied troops under cannon fire.

The rare exercises with artillery brought a crop of accidents. When some regular artillerymen thought to try in a chalk pit "near Mr Unthank's" the old brass cannon, stored in Norwich reputedly since the days of Kett, several of them burst, one sending a lump of metal three-quarters of a mile. A soldier of the Lynn Legion lost his thumb when a spark ignited residual powder in the fieldpiece he was reloading, ejecting the ramrod as a missile. But the worst accident reported was at Cromer when the battery there was exercising in front of a crowd of onlookers, firing grape and cannister at a target on the beach. One wayward ball struck first the battery commander on the foot and then passed on to hit, of all people, the local surgeon whose leg required amputation.

The second phase of full inspections of all units took place in the late Spring of 1804. By then all units had had some chance to settle down, many had served at Yarmouth, and some had participated in exercises on more than troop or company scale. Accordingly the inspections by Metzner and another colonel were considerably more rigorous. Units were classified into three classes:

> 1. Corps that are in the greatest state of forwardness in discipline so as to be fit to be employed in any situation to which Volunteer Corps

can be called. [Which might itself be thought a somewhat equivocal assessment.]

2. Such Corps as are in a state of improvement and tho' not equal to the first class yet are competent to ordinary duties and may be employed in garrison or on guard of prisoner convoys and other services of that nature.

3. Such Corps as from their backward state of discipline or unpromising appearance with respect to improvement can be considered as only fit to remain at home in aid of the Civil Power in the preservation and security of the internal tranquillity of the country.

About half the cavalry reached the first category and most of the rest were placed in the second, only one unit, the Marshland troop, which shortly after disappears from the records, being left in the third. But the state of the infantry was much less satisfactory. In the highest category appear only the large corps of the Blickling & Gunton Riflemen; the Norwich Volunteer Infantry Battalion under John Patteson; the Norwich Riflemen under Richard Bacon; the Yarmouth Volunteer Infantry under William Gould; and the Swaffham company of infantry under Robert Ottley, both the latter two officers being former regulars. The large Norwich Regiment under Robert Harvey and a fair number of other infantry units including the main Lynn units were placed in the second class, but the bad news was that no less than fifteen units including the whole of Hamond's Freebridge Lynn battalion were in category three.

The problem of geographical separation of the country units was emphasised in the case of the Tenth Battalion which was also commanded by Ottley. Whereas his own Swaffham company had been placed in the first class, that from Downham was in the second and his other scattered companies from Marham, Mundford and Barton were in the third. The inability of isolated companies to train with the rest of their battalions and to share effectively in the services of a drill sergeant from the regulars was probably the reason why most of the poor gradings applied to units from the smaller towns and from the countryside. Indeed in the case of Freebridge Lynn it is hard to see how even two of its individual companies could often get together. The first company consisted of 78 men of whom 74 came from three adjacent parishes (and may have been mainly Hamond's own tenantry) but the second and third drew from fourteen and eight parishes respectively, the average parish contingent being just seven men. Only one parish contributed more than twelve and some just one. Given that the men would have to walk to their point of muster there could have been very little time for company training.

In March Bulwer was pressing Townshend for a promotion to brigadier general. He had heard that one such was to be put over every three thousand or so volunteers in the event of active service. He would like the rank but in any event would not wish to serve under another of that rank who had an inferior date of seniority as colonel. As several times before he reminded Townshend of his efforts on behalf of the county over a period of many years. In July 1804 both he and Money were taken onto the staff of the Eastern Military Region under General Sir James Craig at which point Bulwer was indeed promoted to brigadier general. He was to command all Norfolk volunteer infantry and fixed his headquarters at Norwich but within weeks he was posted to Liverpool to command all volunteers there. Although stationed at Liverpool until his death in 1807 and now of general rank in the volunteers he remained in command of the Second Norfolk Cavalry. Thus in January 1805 he was once again lobbying Townshend for promotion, this time to full colonel in the regular army so as not to be outranked in Norfolk by Colonel Thomas Hulton of the 5th Norfolk Battalion who had achieved that rank when formerly in the militia. Bulwer's command of Norfolk infantry was taken over by a regular, Major General Milner. General Money was placed in charge not only of the Norfolk yeomanry cavalry but those of Suffolk as well, and perhaps all within the military district. He remained colonel of the Eastern Norfolk Cavalry but presumably active command was exercised by his lieutenant colonel.

9. Volunteers from 1805 - Decline and Fall

By the Spring of 1805 the Norfolk volunteers as a whole were probably as well prepared for combat as they would ever be although numbers appearing on parade were declining and at least two of the smallest units (Dereham infantry and Marshland cavalry) had already disbanded. Even in April 1804 Townshend had reported that there had been "considrable defalcations" from the original enrolled strengths. The Yarmouth cavalry who had resigned in 1804 were in 1805 being pursued in the courts for the return of their equipment which they maintained was their personal property. In the Commander in Chief's plans to meet an invasion in Kent or Sussex about half the volunteers of the country were to be ordered to march (or be conveyed in wagons or by canal) to the London area to operate in conjunction with the regular and militia forces. But all those in the Eastern Military District - Norfolk, Suffolk, part of Essex, Huntingdon and Cambridgeshire- were to stay put. While this can be construed as a means of reinforcement to the otherwise weak forces under General Craig in the event of a diversionary raid by the enemy into Essex or Suffolk, one must suspect that inspection reports had not inspired confidence in the volunteers' ability to operate on anything like equal terms with regulars. The entire volunteer force for the five counties comprising the district was given as approximately 20,000, suggesting that a material part of Norfolk's paper strength of some 7,000 must have been excluded as ineffective.

More promisingly the energetic General Money had begun experimenting at the end of 1804 with mobile artillery which he believed could be served by volunteers. Learning that a new type of lightweight cannon had been developed by the Navy Board of Works he advocated fitting 9 or 12 pounder guns on the back of Norfolk 60 cwt. corn wagons, strengthened longitudinally to stand the recoil, and able to move relatively swiftly to threatened points on the coast or to vital bridges and defended crossings of the marshes. An alternative use would be to provide inshore fire cover for coastal craft threatened by privateers. Farmers would be paid a retainer to provide their carts on demand and refitting the guns would take only an hour. He reported on experiments carried out in his own grounds, attended by officers from the Royal Artillery, where the feasibility of the scheme was tested. It was found that a gun could be fired with a full charge without disturbing its aim or driving the cart back by recoil, and that traversing the piece by moving the front end of the wagon was fully as swift as was possible with conventional fieldpieces. Townshend duly passed on his suggestions to the War Office, but it would appear that the ideas were never followed up.

Whatever the reality, the news that Napoleon had marched east followed a few months later by that of Trafalgar persuaded many that invasion would never come. It may be questioned whether the less militaristic gentlemen of the county were not losing their enthusiasm for playing soldiers even before that. Anthony Hamond refrained from his normal annual visit to Bath in the summers of 1803 and 1804 but, although a battalion commander, was there again in 1805 when his unit was left in charge of his second in command. Volunteers regularly took part in parades on occasions such as the King's birthday but, these appearances apart, far less appears about them in the newspapers after 1804. No progress had been made, if indeed any could have been, in welding together some of the scattered battalions. In February the commanding officer of the 2nd Battalion (Fakenham area) was declining to submit battalion returns saying that "this regiment is no collected corps" and joined together only when embodied. The government too had lost some of its earlier qualified enthusiasm for volunteers. For 1804 the figures for troops within Great Britain are given as 87,000 regulars, 80,000 militia and 380,000 yeomanry and volunteers. The huge size of the voluntary forces drew much criticism as detrimental to recruitment to the regulars either directly or via the militia.

Townshend's correspondence with the government during this year is much concerned with money and difficult decisions on promotions. Major Charles Laton of the Tunstead & Happing Yeomanry wished to be a lieutenant colonel in the 3rd Norfolk Cavalry Regiment. He had been twenty years in the army, ten in the militia and now ten in the yeomanry so was it not time for some recognition? Lieutenant Colonel Robert Harvey commanding the 7th Norfolk Infantry (the Norwich Regiment) was a particularly demanding correspondent. In April he was pointing out that his unit received allowances on a lower scale than Patteson's Norwich Battalion (due to its later date of formation) and as a result his men were resigning and then joining Patteson's unit. His men could not do without their pay when training and the Norwich fund would soon be exhausted. So could the regiment please be embodied for a thirty day period and march to Yarmouth so that they would receive pay from the government?

A month later Harvey was asking whether he could not be promoted full colonel. He pointed out how he had founded the Norwich Light Horse, then become commander of the former third regiment of militia shortly before it was broken up, and now had many of his family serving as volunteers .... and he had always been a strong supporter of King, Church and Constitution. He was still asking in 1807, and persistence paid for he received his coveted promotion in that year a few weeks before Townshend's death. An interesting sidelight on Harvey's unit came when the men of the grenadier company wanted their officer dismissed on the grounds that he swore at them. Many of them, it was said, " are above the lower ranks of life" and were not used to such treatment.

The Holkham troop in 1805 were still pursuing a claim for refund of horse duty which they had to pay for 1803 because as late starters they had not got in the requisite amount of training before the end of that year although they had made up for it in 1804. Townshend was sympathetic, as indeed he normally was to all applicants, usually passing the buck by forwarding each difficult application to the Home Secretary. The 9th Battalion went on duty to

Yarmouth in May but found it difficult to persuade the local commissary to pay each man the "marching guinea" which was the normal reward paid for temporary embodiment and service away from home. This may have been because Townshend had authorised the embodiment without informing the local military commander who by now was General Charles Fitzroy. The latter complained at the end of May that he had not been consulted on several embodiments; now he doubted that the two Southrepps companies should go, as they wished, to Cromer for ten days on paid embodiment. It was too close to home and there would be no other troops there with whom to exercise.

In June both the Wells and Fakenham companies applied to go to Cromer for no less than twenty-one days but the plan had to be altered as Cromer, with only five inns, could hardly accommodate them all and Fakenham decided they would rather go to Lynn. Meanwhile the Yarmouth battalion was permitted to be embodied at home for its annual training. After this more and more companies found it attractive to do their embodied training without leaving home, although they presumably lost their marching guinea in consequence.

Numbers were falling off at parades and days of exercise. Townshend favoured reducing the establishment where there were substantial shortfalls in the number of effective troops as this would enable the officer establishment to be reduced as well, with excess officers forced out. But some units still wanted to expand. Joseph Taylor commanding the Lynn Legion was always expansionist and in June wanted to recruit more artillerymen. Also, as he now had two troops of cavalry and three companies of riflemen as well as his artillery, could he please be promoted to lieutenant colonel? Townshend assented since other corps had shrunk but pointed out that Taylor's own cavalry were under strength.

In August it was noted that the Norwich Riflemen had re-recruited back to establishment after a bad period "... in consequence of a melancholy accident which occurred while practising ball firing." Their commander pointed out later in the year that his unit had been virtually self-supporting financially since formation but now funds had dried up and they needed similar allowances to other infantry units if they were to carry on. At the end of the year North Walsham wanted to expand from two to three companies, but only if the rate of allowances could be substantially enhanced. Commanders of the more scattered battalions were applying for horse allowances for their adjutants who were supposed to visit all training. And by the end of the year four more units had disbanded including the Holkham and Twyford cavalry troops and the Twyford and Barningham companies of infantry.

William Windham of Felbrigg MP, a former Secretary at War and latterly commander of the Felbrigg Volunteer Infantry and the 4th Battalion of Norfolk Volunteer Infantry, had from the beginning been the chief critic of the volunteer movement. His idea for invasion defence was an "armed peasantry" living at home but ready with arms to rise up and fight as guerrillas, somewhat the same concept as underlay the Home Guards in 1940, and possibly derived from General Money with whom he was acquainted. In the summer of 1803 he had in fact recruited his small company around Felbrigg on just such lines. As a convinced aristocrat he regarded the volunteer movement as it developed as extremely dangerous, tending to create "a revolutionary democracy of armed men", taking too many away from useful labour, causing confusion amongst all ranks, and serving as a bad influence on the morals of the people. More practically he regretted that its size was detrimental to regular recruitment, and scoffed at the large numbers of over-promoted volunteer officers in fine uniforms parading around London. Neither he nor many regular officers were confident of the behaviour of amateurs when ordered to fight in line opposite the trained and experienced soldiers of Napoleon. In 1803 his views aroused little sympathy except among regular soldiers, but as time went on the size and expense of the volunteer organisation was found increasingly burdensome.

By early 1806, not only was there no prospect of invasion in even the medium term but, following the death of Pitt in January, there was a different government. Windham, now Secretary of State for War and the Colonies, determined to cut the volunteer army down to size. The national returned strength of volunteers in 1804 of 380,000 fell appreciably in successive years but it was still over 300,000 in 1806 and costing each year something approaching one million pounds. Moreover that was only about half the cost to the nation for an equal amount had in all probability been provided by public subscriptions or service without pay. Windham wanted the bulk of the labouring population to be available for recruitment into the regular army and not, as he put it, "shut up within those volunteer corps", although nevertheless trained in arms via the militia or some similar organisation.

He contrived that volunteers pay and allowances should be much reduced and that there should be no future clothing allowances. Gentlemen volunteers could continue in volunteer units, where they would be protected from mixing with the common soldiery. "Nothing in future would exempt any man from the general training [which he proposed] but his becoming a volunteer at his own expense, the advantage of which to him would be that he could train and fight (if occasion required it) in his own corps instead of being obliged to join the regulars."

Windham's proposals were carried into law as the General Training Act at the cost of considerable dismay amongst the volunteer units. Norfolk prepared to put the training provisions of the new law into effect. It was estimated that some 18,000 men in the county were due to be trained and in April 1807 just over 600 men were drawn by ballot to begin their twenty-four days training. But Windham had already left the War Office when the government fell in the previous month and it is probable that nobody whatever received the training that the Act had called for.

So long as Windham was in office the volunteers were actively discouraged, particularly by the withdrawal of allowances. Nevertheless the majority of the Norfolk volunteers agreed to continue their services under the new terms even though the militia ballot had been suspended for two years, so removing any need for ballot exemption which many held was the principal motive for remaining a volunteer. However the withdrawal of most allowances for clothing coupled with the exhaustion of the town's funds raised for the volunteers brought about the demise of one of the county's more efficient units when the Lynn volunteer battalion, the 1st Norfolks, voted in the autumn of 1806 to disband. Their clothing was worn out and the residual allowance was quite inadequate to replace it. To save money even the regimental drums had been sacrificed. Taylor of the Lynn Legion, aware of the impending break up before it occurred, wrote to enquire whether he would be granted a fresh clothing allowance if he recruited any of the men into his corps. Several less satisfactory units also disappeared from the records in that year including the whole of the 11th Norfolks, Anthony Hamond's less than enthusiastic unit, all the officers resigning in a body in October.

The usual pattern with the smaller and more isolated units which broke up was that the senior officer resigned, sometimes because of leaving the district, sometimes for no stated reason, and once at least because he had taken holy orders. Then if Townshend could find no eligible person to succeed he would recommend that the unit be disbanded. Five companies in rural Norfolk appear to have gone in this way. When the commander of Harleston's two companies left the area not only were the town's troops disbanded but the 8th Battalion, which he also commanded, was broken up to survive only as three independent companies.

In the case where the commander had taken orders, the second Wells company, he had persuaded the other officers to resign as well before Townshend was even aware of what was happening. Those men of the company "to whom pay is an object" would join "other corps", probably the town's other company; the remainder, " all respectable tradesmen", left the volunteers though the retiring commander was sure that they would gladly take up arms again in the event of any emergency. The 2nd Norfolk Battalion, of which this Wells company had formed part, continued on the War Office registers notwithstanding that three of its original seven companies had been disbanded but its nominal commander continued to refuse all requests to render returns because, as he repeated, he had at all times left the separate companies to administer themselves.

The remaining units continued with periodic training and also to garrison Yarmouth, Lynn and sometimes other towns on a rota basis each summer. But as in 1805 this activity was more connected with drawing pay for a week or longer of embodiment than it was a reaction to any external threat. Moreover the practice of letting units perform their period of embodiment "without leaving their homes" was extended even to the larger such as the Norwich Regiment. No doubt this saved cost and dislocation but it can scarcely have improved the efficiency of the units.

At the inspections of March 1806 the numbers appearing on parade for those companies still in existence was substantially less in most cases than at the first muster of the same units in late 1803. The number noted as absent without leave, up to a quarter of nominal strength in the case of the cavalry, is depressing while most units were well below establishment. The returns at different dates cannot always be compared safely: Appendix 1 shows only rank and file present or stated as effective. Between ten and fifteen per cent must be added for the full complement of officers, sergeants, drummers, trumpeters etc whose absences from parades are not usually noted. But despite uncertainties over the basis of the returns the severe falling off from 1803 to 1806 is obvious.

Lord Castlereagh, successor to Windham as Secretary of State and no less a sceptic concerning the volunteers, gave some encouragement to the volunteers in May 1807 when first in office to avoid a total collapse. Some allowances were revived and the inspecting officers whom Windham had withdrawn were reinstated. The new climate was warm enough for the ever optimistic Taylor of the Lynn Legion to ask permission to raise an extra company and efforts were made to revive the broken up 8th Battalion by recruitment adequate to justify an adjutant and a lieutenant colonel to command. In September Townshend died, active to the last, to be succeeded as lord lieutenant by William Harbord. Unfortunately the correspondence for the next six months is missing but it seems doubtful that the spirit of revival lasted for long.

In 1808 things were going on as before with surviving units applying for their brief embodiments at Yarmouth or some other town or at home but that summer Castlereagh produced radical proposals for reorganisation of the local defence forces which passed into law in July 1808. By this legislation was created the Local Militia, a purely infantry force selected by ballot within counties, to be attached for purposes of training to the regiments of the militia proper, the members of which were to serve for four years certain. The volunteers would be retained, but only so far as they were prepared and able to pay for themselves. This it was assumed would limit their ranks to the yeomanry and to the better off who would not care to serve in the militia with the poorer classes. Castlereagh assumed that infantry volunteers would come preponderantly from the towns while the landed classes in the country would provide the officers for both the yeomanry and the Local Militia. The members of the Local Militia would be paid while in training and as a result it was expected that many persons at present in volunteer units would transfer to the new organisation.

This was enough for many of the remaining Norfolk volunteer infantry units. All of some and a major part of some others immediately agreed to transfer. Others disbanded, including the Yarmouth infantry and the rifle company of the Lynn Legion, but others yet were still prepared to stick it out as volunteers. Nearly all of Patteson's Norwich Battalion transferred but Harvey could not persuade more than a minority of his Norwich Regiment to move with him. As a result he resigned from its command and another officer succeeded. Harvey maintained that he should then take over command of the Local Militia battalion which drew its men from Norwich but because Patteson, now one of Norwich's MPs, had brought over more men he received the appointment. In consequence there was for some years a feud between the two men who had earlier been political allies within Norwich as they later were again.

It was the new lord lieutenant's responsibility to reorganise the county's forces from a voluntary basis to the balloted and hence ultimately compulsory Local Militia which was to number about seven thousand of all ranks. In doing this he had more problems than those of Norwich to encounter but the process appears to have been relatively smooth. In the summer of 1809 the press reported the establishment of twenty-eight day summer training camps for the six new regiments, spread between Norwich, Yarmouth, Lynn and Swaffham. By the following summer the references were to a training period of only twenty days 'The regimental commanders included Patteson, Harbord himself (from 1810 Lord Suffield) and Colonel Edmund Wodehouse, formerly a junior volunteer officer.

Patteson's regiment was the 2nd East Norfolk Local Militia. Amongst his family papers deposited in the Norfolk Record Office are invoices and correspondence concerning the initial clothing and equipping of the unit. Clearly one incentive for transferring was the opportunity for a complete replacement of kit at government expense. Altogether close to £1,500 was spent on providing every non-commissioned member of the new regiment with new coat, waistcoat, breeches, hat, shirt, gaiters, stock and knapsack, with sashes for the sergeants and one flag, "richly emblazoned" for the unit's colours. The government's allowance for the 700 privates, 33 sergeants and 15 drummers would have come to over £1,800 although it is unclear just how much was claimed and paid. While it might seem that the colonel was to realise a profit of some three hundred pounds the costs recorded do not include any allowance for the new boots which would surely have been required.

Some of the volunteers hung on grimly. In July 1809 the remnants of the Norwich Regiment were told that there would be no further allowances for clothing and were asked to consider forming a new corps in the Local Militia. But the response was that they preferred to stay as they were and would do so until they were forcibly disbanded or their clothing wore out. A return for 1812 shows that there were still a few volunteers in Norfolk apart from the yeomanry but several of the units still registered with an establishment had not rendered any return of effectives and some of these may in fact have ceased to exist.

The end came in March of the following year when the remaining corps of infantry volunteers were finally disbanded, depositing their arms in depots, and receiving the thanks of the Prince Regent for their years of service. But only two months later the Local Militia itself was effectively brought to an end. For as Napoleon was driven out of Germany by Russia, Austria and a

65

resurgent Prussia the Local Militia was ordered to hand over its arms and accoutrements which, together with those handed in by the volunteers, were to be shipped from Yarmouth to Hamburg to arm the new German levies.

Only the yeomanry remained as any form of local defence force, and were to remain so for many years to come in the absence of any effective county constabulary. It was probably always more fun to be a trooper in the yeomanry than a footslogger in the infantry. The Yarmouth yeomanry drew up and saluted Lord Nelson on his departure from Yarmouth after his triumphal visit to that town in 1801 and then escorted his carriage all the way to Lowestoft. It was the Yarmouth yeomanry too who participated in the first races held on the North Denes where stands the present racecourse, competing for a cup presented by their own Captain Lacon.

In February 1809 when the troopers of the Norwich Light Horse were finishing their exercise on Mulbarton Common the stag hounds in full pursuit crossed their path. The men immediately joined the chase which lasted a further three hours before the terrified stag was taken alive at Mangreen. But there were also more serious moments. In 1814 the cavalry of the Lynn Legion were involved in putting down the serious rioting of sailors which occurred in the town over two days in April. The last recorded account of yeomanry activity before 1820, apart from parades on King's Birthdays, is for the summer of 1816 when they were called out to deal with riots in Norwich and a number of locations in West Norfolk.

10.   Reflections

It had been an inglorious falling off for the yeomanry, a miserable ending for the volunteer infantry, but the great war against Napoleon had been won. None of these forces, nor the militia and fencibles, had seen any service more active than guarding prisoners of war or the intimidation of rioters. Had twenty years expenditure of time and money been remotely worthwhile?

Unless one takes the extreme view that Britain would have benefited by being conquered by the French the answer as regards the militia and fencibles must undoubtedly be that, however wearisome their part, it was an essential role in the country's defence in providing a full time home army which, after its initial training, should have proved at least as effective in combat as any other unbloodied formation at its first time in action. Only its existence enabled the high command to mobilise and despatch the expeditionary forces which took part in the campaigns in the West Indies, in India, in Egypt and on the Continent in the Netherlands, Germany, Denmark, Italy and above all in the Peninsula. That the success achieved in these was uneven until the final years was not the fault of the militia or fencibles. Only the expansion and replenishment of the militia and the raising of the parallel supplementary militia, Army of Reserve and Permanent Additional Force eventually provided the reservoir of trained men who could be induced to refill and eventually expand the ranks of the regular army as the long war drew on. Norfolk certainly provided its full share of all these forces as well as of direct regular recruits.

The value of the volunteers is more questionable. If the yeomanry are considered solely in their initial role as an area police force to deal with riot and unrest, a species of White Guard recruited from and acting for the propertied classes to intimidate any radical or republican elements in the population or simply to repress the hungry and desperate, they can be seen as a qualified success. There was plenty of hunger and distress amongst the Norfolk population during the wars, especially in 1795 and 1800 after crop failures which occasioned intermittent local rioting, and there was anti-ballot rioting too, but no widespread disturbances until 1816. Yet when rioting did occur the authorities were reluctant to call out the yeomanry, preferring instead to use regular troops or militia from another county when available who might strike a better balance between sympathy with the rioters on the one hand and brutal repression on the other. For example in 1795 Townshend called on the Pembrokeshire militia, then stationed in Norfolk, to discourage food rioters at Wells. Better an indecisive outcome than Bulwer with his ball cartridge and dead bodies in the streets although Townshend noted in a letter to the Home Secretary that the countryside was quiet where troops of yeomanry existed.

Richard Glover argues that the sheer existence of the mass of volunteers in 1803/05 had an important deterrent effect on the French. He is impressed by the importance of the role which the duke of York, commander in chief, expected them to play in the defence of London, and by the numbers from other parts of the country than Norfolk that were considered by inspecting officers to be fit to stand in line with regular troops. However his argument is based less on that than on the indirect effect of their sheer numbers. Taken together with the regulars and militia the forces defending the country in 1805, the time of the greatest danger, exceeded half a million, nearly two thirds of them volunteers. However low an opinion Napoleon might have had of the volunteer element, it inevitably must have entered his calculations, and explains why he was aiming to land more than one hundred and fifty thousand French troops, a force more than three times that considered necessary by the French in the invasion plans of earlier wars. And the difficulties created by the need to organise the transport and shipping of so many men to cross the formidable barrier of the channel must be one reason why the actual attempt was never made.

If numbers were what counted Norfolk's contribution was scarcely adequate as a share of the national total. It is not entirely clear that the volunteer total ever quite reached the three-quarters of the county requirement under the Defence Act of 1803; Fortescue says it did not although it must have come fairly close before boredom set in, subscription funds ran out, and the number of effectives dropped off. Norfolk's quota for the "old" militia was about one thousand out of a total of thirty thousand for England as a whole, say three and one half per cent. Its contribution to the volunteers at the height of their strength was only some seven thousand out of three hundred thousand (excluding Ireland and Scotland) or not much more than two per cent. The country's population had been rising fast since the militia quotas were originally set, and rising faster outside Norfolk than within, but it does seem that volunteer enthusiasm in the county was less than elsewhere and depended far more on local leadership than on any mass movement in the population as a whole. This is especially true of the period from 1794 to 1797 when there was substantial opposition amongst some of the county's leaders to the war and hence to any participation in voluntary defence at all. Norfolk seems to have contributed its full share of yeomanry, but the infantry, inevitably centred on towns, could not draw effectively on the mass of agricultural labourers which was such a large element of Norfolk's population. These latter were left to the mercy of the ballot and to compulsory full time service if chosen.

Much of the writing in recent years concerned with the history of the volunteer movement in the Napoleonic period has concentrated on who volunteered and why. The latter part of the question can seldom be answered other than speculatively. The former for Norfolk is easier. The yeomanry were also principally the tenantry of those local magnates who were enthusiastic for defence and for local law and order. They were by definition the better off in their districts since they had to be able to provide both free time and a horse. The infantry undoubtedly included men who could not afford to spend time training unless paid, but most must have come from towns, whether large or small, because most infantry units were centred there and the lack of transport for those from remoter districts would have prevented their frequent attendance to be trained even if time had been available. And in towns, especially the smaller towns, it was the tradesmen and shopkeepers and their staff who comprised the bulk of the male population of military age. In the ports of Yarmouth, Lynn and Wells the seamen were already either in the navy or at sea in merchant vessels, while the longshoremen and fishermen were drawn to, if not forced into, the sea fencibles.

The biggest uncommitted reserve of men may have been amongst the Norwich manufacturers' labourers, and certainly Norwich did not provide volunteers in such a large proportion to its total population as did the two ports. Norwich with a population of some 36,000 provided 1,500 volunteers at most or about four per cent. Lynn, with a population of about 10,000 provided some 900 or nine per cent including sea fencibles but not including men serving in the navy. Yarmouth's population was about 16,000 and its volunteer force some 600 at its maximum but the number of sea fencibles is not known. If they were only equal to Lynn's 300 then their percentage would be five and a half. That the town men were tradesmen is shown not only from Ewart's analysis of volunteers from certain Norwich parishes in the 1790s but also from Lynn. In 1795 Edward Everard, their commander, stated specifically that the majority of his men were journeymen who could not spare time to train without pay as often as training was desirable. In debates in 1797 and 1798 about the circumstances in which volunteers might be called out for full time service it was stated more than once that men would not volunteer if they believed that they would be called out in circumstances other than actual invasion as they feared the ruin of their businesses.

Under the plans to resist invasion in 1805 the Norfolk volunteers were not to leave East Anglia and do not seem to have been expected to leave the county unless an actual landing took place in Essex or Suffolk. Left to defend Norfolk with only minimal assistance from the regular and militia garrisons, how might they have made out had a landing in fact been made in the county by the French or their Dutch allies? Given the known dispositions of the enemy there was no chance whatever that Norfolk might be the scene of the main invasion but a landing in force by, say, fifteen thousand men leaving from the Texel or the Scheldt was a possibility. There would have been no object and much difficulty in landing any such force in the remoter parts of the county's shore, even unopposed. The northern Norfolk coast is too exposed for anchored transports while the primary object of any diversionary landing must have been to draw off forces from the south by threatening a vulnerable region. So the probability would be of a landing designed swiftly to capture a port, Yarmouth being the obvious and indeed the only possibility, and to capture or at least threaten Norwich. This was exactly what Townshend, Money and the various staff officers all foresaw. But, although the War Office accepted that field fortifications at the marsh crossings would be essential, nothing was in fact done. Perhaps, as with London, it was felt that such fortifications could be erected very swiftly by agricultural labourers aided by horse ploughs, and that no good would be done to civilian morale by premature construction.

In this scenario, which implies that naval defence had failed and that the invading fleet had successfully navigated into Yarmouth Roads, the first actions would probably have been on the beaches around Corton to the south or Caister to the north of Yarmouth itself to avoid the batteries close to the town. Alternatively one can accept Money's prediction of Pakefield or Solebay. Opposed landings are difficult, and were more difficult then before the days of specialised landing craft when the beaches had to be reached under oars. But they were not impossible and were made, as when British forces landed in Egypt in the face of French resistance. The Yarmouth garrison varied in strength but never exceeded two and a half thousand, the majority volunteers. It would have been at the moment of landing that they would have had their best chances of success. Had the invaders got ashore, and especially if they succeeded in landing even some light artillery, there was little to stop them from taking the town and the whole of Flegg if landing to the north or Lowestoft and Lothing if to the south. The problem would then have been, as Money foresaw, stopping them at the crossings of the marshes from reaching the firmer ground to the north or south of Norwich. Nor is it impossible that they would have had the initiative and ability to make use of the rivers themselves as a means to penetrate the local defences.

In the absence of General Money's wagon borne field guns the defenders had little available in the way of artillery, and the possibility of volunteers on their own holding a determined enemy at what Money described as the "passes" into mainland Norfolk would seem to have been thin. It would be then that the deficiencies in their training would have been most exposed. As Money repeatedly emphasised, much of eastern Norfolk – and for that matter a good deal of England including eastern Kent – was quite unsuitable for conventional cavalry operations. It was too enclosed and Money, scornful of the use of pure cavalry in such close country, was an advocate of mixed units of horse and foot. Mounted units he held should be accompanied by companies of pioneers and of sharpshooters who could break gaps in hedges and fire from cover and he had recruited auxiliary companies to this end. In this he was in agreement with Townshend himself whose Norfolk Rangers were similarly, though not identically, organised and also with other volunteer units such as the Lynn Legion which incorporated both riflemen and light artillery. Townshend's people were indeed trained to ride two-up so that the cavalry could transport the riflemen swiftly to a scene of action. Both Townshend and Money would no doubt have preferred that all cavalrymen were trained in fighting dismounted, but this did not happen in any yeomanry corps, probably because the yeomanry, volunteers and not always amenable to discipline, were more interested in wielding their sabres than in getting off their horses, a characteristic of horsemen in all wars, at least at their outset.

The most useful troops amongst the volunteers would in all probability have been the riflemen whether those in the composite cavalry units or the various companies of sharpshooters, riflemen, and light infantry provided, a big proviso, that their training in marksmanship had been adequate. Both Townshend and Money had experience in North America where conventional operations with lines of infantry face to face often proved impossible in wooded and broken countryside, and it was probably easier to train countrymen volunteers in irregular tactics than in parade ground drill and manoeuvres. When supporting the Norwich Riflemen in their quest for increased allowances Townshend wrote in October 1805, "I cannot avoid expressing my opinion that of all descriptions of volunteers the irregulars will be the most essentially serviceable in the defence of the country".

The least effective volunteer troops of all, when not protected by field fortifications, were likely to have been the companies of conventional infantry armed with muskets. The essence of parade ground drill was to train men to get up close to an enemy and there to stand in line and fire at him at short range, short range giving the only hope of a hit with the standard musket. This took enormous courage, great discipline and perhaps invincible ignorance or callousness on the part of the soldiers who sometimes took horrendous casualties, especially if the enemy possessed cannon. Few units behaved well at their first such experience and commanders took care if possible to mix new soldiers with hardened veterans. The annals of military history are full of stories of inexperienced troops breaking and fleeing in the face of smaller numbers of a determined enemy. Moreover the French in these wars attacked in column, tactically possibly disastrous in the face of adequately trained troops who might manoeuvre to fire at the column's flank, but terrifying when first encountered. It is hard to imagine the Norwich infantry, the largest formed units in the county, standing up to this when first met despite all their expertise in the calmer conditions of a field day at Hellesdon. It is harder still to see the other Norfolk infantry battalions getting near the scene of action in time or being able to manoeuvre at all other than as isolated companies. The chances of Norwich being successfully defended by the volunteers must have been poor once the invading force had got ashore.

Money's hope and Windham's dream of an armed peasantry, equipped with rifles and trained in marksmanship and fieldcraft, which would rise up against any invader in defence of their homes must equally be an illusion. Of course guerrillas can be effective in pinning down large quantities of enemy troops and even in preventing them from conducting major operations. Spain in these same wars showed the possibilities. But guerrillas need a countryside more rugged than Norfolk's to operate successfully; mountain, thick forest or remote refuges and an enemy with long lines of communication through a large and comparatively empty countryside are essential. Thus the Spaniards could hold out against the French in 1810, the Boers against the British in 1901, the Yugoslavs against the Germans in 1942, and the Vietcong against the Americans in the 1960s to cite only a few of many examples, but hardly the Norfolk labourers against the French in 1805 even though the latter had yet to learn the tactics of reprisal against civilians which have become the standard response to guerrilla tactics. They soon learnt in Spain. Moreover guerrillas alone seldom win wars. In any case Money's picture of embattled farmers armed with fowling pieces did not match the facts. The majority of the volunteers came from the towns, large and small. Some farmers (and no doubt some poachers) had suitable weapons, but most farm labourers did not and the gentry were not anxious that they should acquire any.

So it must be concluded that, apart from swelling the numbers of troops available on paper, and so perhaps helping to impress Napoleon's spies, the volunteer movement in Norfolk at least was of little practical value as a defence against invasion. Socially it probably did have value for a short period after 1803 in providing a practical outlet for patriotic enthusiasm and helping to unite the populace in a common effort. The charge that the main reason for volunteering was to avoid the militia and allied ballots must have been valid for some but had it been universal there would have been more volunteers than there were and more evenly spread over the county. More of the volunteers would have been those, as at Wells, to whom "pay was an object" and fewer would have been the respectable shopkeepers and tradesmen of the same town who presumably could have afforded to pay for a substitute rather than accept the ballot.

The parades to receive colours or on the King's birthday were popular as were the mock battles in 1804, always attended by numerous spectators. Nearly every parade in those days was followed by a dinner for all participants with rousing patriotic songs and loyal toasts, reported at length in the local papers. Only when the immediate invasion threat departed and was replaced by the reality of a further long and at times seemingly endless war did the enthusiasm drain away. Then officers resigned, units were broken up, and training fell into arrears. Only the most enthusiastic or forceful of the local leaders could keep the volunteer spirit going in the face of official opposition. From the time the introduction of the Local Militia turned local soldiering into a compulsory service it was only the most determined of commanders who could inspire the rumps of their units to hold together without pay or allowances through to the final disbandment of 1813.

Appendices

NORFOLK VOLUNTEERS 1794-1815
1. YEOMANRY CAVALRY

(Allocation of troops/companies to regiments as in April 1804)

	Dates of acceptance 1794/1801	1802/......	Commanders in December 1803	Troops 1803	Yarmouth 1803/4	Grade 1804	1799	Rank & file 1803	1806	1812	Notes
First Norfolk Cavalry			F M Lord Townshend*								
Norfolk Rangers	Sep 1794		F M Lord Townshend*	2	Yes	1	99	80	53	N/R	Mixed cavalry & sharpshooters
Holkham	Jul 1798	Sep 1803	Lt Col Thomas Coke*	1	Yes	2	74	43	Disbanded		
Smithdon & Brothercross	Jul 1798	Aug 1803	Capt William Hoste	1	Yes	1	43	26	21	N/R	
Marshland		Oct 1803	Capt D Coates	1		3		30	Disbanded		
Lynn Legion	Jul 1798	Oct 1802	Maj Joseph Taylor*	2	Yes	2	41	89	30	N/R	Plus riflemen and field artillery. Refused to join 1st Norfolk Regt.
Second Norfolk Cavalry			Col W Earle Bulwer*								
South Erpingham & Eynesford	Mar 1797	Oct 1802	Col W Earle Bulwer*	1	Yes	2	40	42	24	278	Heydon infantry associated
South Greenhoe		Jul 1803	Capt Robert Wilson*	1	Yes			40	7		
Clackclose/Downham	Nov 1796	Sep 1803	Capt W Lee	1	Yes		96	47	N/R		
1st East Dereham	Oct 1794	Oct 1802	Capt J Hope	1	Yes		60	60	33		
2nd East Dereham	Jun 1798	Oct 1802	Capt J Crispe	1	Yes		36	44	22		
Swaffham		Oct 1802	Capt Richard Johnson	1	Yes		37	34	30		
Hingham	Jun 1794	Oct 1802	Capt Hamond Alpe*	1	Yes		61	64	18		
Twyford?		????	????	1				52	Disbanded		
Third Norfolk Cavalry			Maj Gen John Money*								
Loddon & Claveringham	Dec 1794	Oct 1802	Capt J Smith	1	Yes	1		53	20	311	Plus pioneers & sharpshooters
Wymondham		Sep 1803	Capt Edmund Wodehouse*	1	Yes			60	25		
Blofield & South Walsham	Mar 1795	Oct 1802	Maj James Burroughs*	1	Yes		64	56	40		
Tunstead & Happing	Apr 1795	Oct 1802	Capt Charles Laton	1	Yes		64	67	27		
Yarmouth	Jun 1798	Oct 1802	Maj Edmund K Lacon*	1	Yes		50	55	38		Mass resignation 1804; re-recruited
Norwich Light Horse	Mar 1797	Oct 1802	Maj John Harvey*	2	Yes		59	92	33		
							890	1034	421	589	

NORFOLK VOLUNTEERS 1794-1815
2. VOLUNTEER INFANTRY

	Dates of acceptance 1794/1801 1802/......	Commanders in April 1804	Coys	Yarmouth 1803/4	Grade 1804	Rank & file 1799	1803	1806	1812	Notes
First Norfolk Volunteer Infantry										
King's Lynn	Jun 1794	Aug 1803 Lt Col Edward Everard*	8	Yes	2	208	464			Disbanded 1806
Second Norfolk Volunteer Infantry		Lt Col Francis Bedingfield*								
1st Wells	?1801	Jul 1803 Capt Bloom	1	Yes	3	58	62	59	62	Survived to 1813
2nd Wells (sharpshooters)		Sep 1803 Capt Hill	1		3		42			Disbanded 1806
Fakenham		Aug 1803 Maj Thomas M Case	2	Yes	2		140	34	126	Survived to 1813
Little Walsingham		Sep 1803 Capt Adcock	1		2		60	37		Disbanded 1808
Twyford		Sep 1803 Capt Savory	1		3					Gone by 1805
Ryburgh		Sep 1803 Capt Francis	1		3		71	25		No trace after 1806
Third Norfolk Volunteer Infantry										
This battalion never formed, but was intended to contain										
Blickling & Gunton Riflemen		Aug 1803 Lt Col W A Harbord*	6	Yes	1		360	274		Probable transfer to Local Militia
Heydon Sharpshooters		Sep 1803 Col W Earle Bulwer*	3		3		180	110		Transferred to Local Militia
Fourth Norfolk Volunteer Infantry		Lt Col William Windham MP*								
Cromer Battery	Jun 1798	Jul 1803 Capt Mickelburg	1		2	55	75	55	63	Survived to 1813
Felbrigg		Sep 1803 Lt Col William Windham MP*	1		3		62	51		Disbanded 1808
Southrepps		Aug 1803 Capt Woodhouse	2		3		120	71		Disbanded 1808
Holt		Sep 1803 Capt Hewett	2		2		115	82		Probable transfer to Local Militia
North Walsham Light Infantry		Jul 1803 Capt Cooper	2	Yes	2	74	39	82		Probable transfer to Local Militia
Fifth Norfolk Volunteer Infantry		Lt Col Thomas Hulton*								
Aylsham Light Infantry		Aug 1803 Maj Collyer	2	Yes	3		204	131		Disbanded 1808
North Elmham		Nov 1803 Capt Hopson	1		3		30	74		Probable Transfer to Local Militia
Hingham	May 1794	Aug 1803 Capt Gillman	1		2		37	61		Transferred to Local Militia
East Dereham		Sep 1803 Capt Luder	1		2		30			Disbanded before May 1805
Sixth Norfolk Volunteer Infantry										
Yarmouth	Jul 1798	Aug 1803 Lt Col William Gould*	6	Yes	1	130	480	395		Disbanded 1808
Seventh Norfolk Volunteer Infantry										
Norwich Regiment		Aug 1803 Lt Col Robert Harvey*	10	Yes	2		760	473	315	Part transferred to Local Militia, remainder survived to 1813
plus unbrigaded but associated										
Norwich Battalion	Apr 1797	May 1803 Lt Col John Patteson*	6	Yes	1	233	312	230		Transferred to Local Militia
Norwich Riflemen		Aug 1803 Maj Richard M Bacon*	3	Yes	1		121	113		N/R Survived to 1813

	Dates of acceptance 1794/1801	1802/......	Commanders in April 1804	Coys	Yarmouth 1803/4	Grade 1804	Rank & file 1799	1803	1806	1812	Notes
Eighth Norfolk Volunteer Infantry			Lt Col John Kerrick*			2					Broken into companies 1806
Loddon		Sep 1803	Maj Mathias	1				62	60	N/R	Survived to 1813
Pulham St Mary		Sep 1803	Capt Webb	1				68	60	N/R	Survived to 1813
Brooke		Sep 1803	Capt Dix	1				60	38		Transferred to Local Militia
Harlesden		Aug 1803	Lt Col John Kerrick*	2				80	71		Disbanded 1806
Ninth Norfolk Volunteer Infantry			Lt Col Thomas J Woodward*			2					
Old Buckenham	Jun 1798	Aug 1803	Lt Col Powell	2	Yes		54	134	62		Transferred to Local Militia
Diss	Jun 1798	Aug 1803	Lt Col Thomas J Woodward*	2	Yes		61	152	N/R	134	Survived to 1813
Thetford	? 1798	Sep 1803	Maj Gill	3			48	171	110		Transferred to Local Militia
Tenth Norfolk Volunteer Infantry			Lt Col Robert Ottley*		(Lynn)						
Swaffham Light Infantry		Aug 1803	Lt Col Robert Ottley*	2		1		134	97		Disbanded 1808
Marham		Oct 1803	Capt Winearle	1		3		58	59		Disbanded 1808
Downham		Sep 1803	Capt Saffery	2		2		110	88		Disbanded 1808
Barton		Sep 1803	Capt Musdell	1		3		60	45		Disbanded 1808
Mundford		Sep 1803	Capt Moseley	1		3		60			Disbanded 1806
Eleventh Norfolk Volunteer Infantry			Lt Col Anthony Hamond*								
Freebridge Lynn & Westacre		Oct 1803	Lt Col Anthony Hamond*	3		3		210			Disbanded 1806
Smithdon		Oct 1803	Capt Henry Styleman*	1		3		78			Disbanded 1806
plus on paper only, otherwise independent,											
South Lynn		Aug 1803	Capt Middleton	1	Yes	2		100			Probably disbanded 1808
Units never brigaded											
Barningham		Sep 1803	????	1				74			No trace after 1805
Honingham		Sep 1803	Capt Beevor	1		3		102	55	100	Survived to 1813
Great Witchingham		Sep 1803	Capt Burrows	1		3		120	N/R		Disbanded 1808
Catton Sharpshooters		Sep 1803	Capt Jeremiah Ives*	1		2		92	87	71	Survived to 1813
Units not reformed in 1803											
See notes											
							921	5889	3196	871	

* = Brief biographical note appears in Appendix 2.

N/R = in existence but no return received

Rank and file totals exclude officers, sergeants, trumpeters, drummers and battalion staff, and where distinguished include only effectives and/or those attending inspection parades.

NOTES ON APPENDIX 1

Attempting to provide a full unit history of the Norfolk volunteer units over the twenty-one years of the wars presents several areas of difficulty:

1 1794 to 1803

The War Office and Norfolk records do not always agree even when both survive for the same period. The difficulty may lie partly in the difference between a unit making a proposal to the lord lieutenant, which might or (rarely) might not be accepted, and the War Office recording the acceptance of that unit. The differences noted are:

> An infantry company at Hingham recorded by War Office in May 1794 but never in the Norfolk copy returns (which cover only 1799 to 1800)

> An infantry company at Attleborough in existence between May 1798 (proposal) and 1800 as recorded in Norfolk returns but apparently recorded by the War Office as though cavalry. Not reformed in 1803.

> A cavalry troop proposed for the hundred of Shropham and Guiltcross in May 1798 and accepted by the War Office in July which failed to attract sufficent volunteers and thus never existed in fact.

> Units of cavalry at Swaffham and infantry at Wells, North Walsham and Thetford which undoubtedly existed from 1798 but for which no War Office acceptance has been traced. The Thetford unit had collapsed by 1800 but the others had not.

Several Norwich parishes formed or attempted to form armed associations in 1798. Those which survived for at least one year were from the following parishes:

St Peter Mancroft
St Stephens
St Andrews (disbanded by 1800)
St George Tombland
St Lawrence (disbanded by 1800)
St Saviours
St Peter Parmentergate (King Street volunteers)

2. Grouping into infantry battalions in 1804

A complete plan of Townshend's proposed grouping appears in PRO HO50/114 but even there some units remained unallocated to battalions. In fact some elements of his plan were never effected while the existence of some battalions was on paper only since the constituent companies were too far apart ever to permit exercise as a combined unit.

3. Dates of disbandment

The precise dates are known only in a minority of cases. Some companies whose officers were still included by the War Office in the official list for a given year may already have been disbanded.

4. Officer appointments

Resignations, new appointments and promotions were frequent. Appendix 1 can provide only a snapshot, taken in December 1803 for the cavalry and April 1804 for the infantry, the months in which the cavalry regiments and the infantry battalions were first defined. Commanders of cavalry troops and infantry companies should have been captains but were sometimes majors where two or more of these units were grouped together. Company size units whose original commanders had subsequently been appointed to regimental or battalion commands with higher rank continued to be listed as commanded by those same officers although in practice a junior must have commanded in drills and exercises.

Many volunteer officers had previously held regular or militia rank. It appears that it was possible to hold either higher or lower volunteer rank than previous regular/militia rank. The latter case has caused some confusion in this work as it must have done in practice. The extreme case is that of Lord Townshend whose army rank was Field Marshall but as commander of the Norfolk Rangers was holding a post such as would normally have rated a rank no higher than major.

APPENDIX 2

NORFOLK'S SENIOR POLITICIANS
AND SOLDIERS DURING THE WARS

Alpe, Hamond: 1763/1823. Of Hardingham. His father, of Little Fransham, was High Sheriff of county in 1758. Militia captain in American war. Commanded Hingham Yeomanry vice Colonel Dillingham, and later 2nd Norfolk Yeomanry Cavalry in 1807 and again after 1817. According to J R Harvey became Colonel of 18th Light Dragoons and served in Peninsula war.

Astley, Sir Jacob: 1756/1817. Of Burgh and later Melton. Baronet. Son of Sir Edward Astley, formerly an MP for the county, who died in 1803. Sir Jacob was a county MP from 1797 until his death in 1817 apart from a short break in 1806/7. Mild Whig. Married King's Lynn heiress whose sister married Edmund Pratt of Ryston. Divisional lieutenant of four hundreds in north Norfolk in 1803 jointly with Henry Jodrell. Captain in East Norfolk Militia 1780-94. Lieutenant Colonel of Norfolk Fencible Dragoons 1794-99.

Bacon, Richard Mackenzie: 1775/1844. Journalist and musician. Editor of the *Norwich Mercury*. Raised and commanded Norwich Riflemen from 1803.

Bedingfield, Francis Philip: Of Denton. Captain in West Norfolk Militia in 1790s. Commanded 2nd Battalion Norfolk Volunteer Infantry from 1804 (Wells area).

Bedingfield, John: Of Ditchingham. Captain in West Norfolk Militia in early 1790s. Applied for colonelcy of 3rd Norfolk Militia in 1799 but did not get it. Commanded Aylsham Volunteers 1804/5.

Bulwer, William Earle: 1754/1807. Of Heydon and Wood Dalling. Professional soldier. In 1794, raised a line regiment in Norwich (106th Foot). Commanded Erpingham & Eynesford Yeomanry from 1797 plus Heydon Volunteer Infantry from 1803. Also Norfolk Provisional Cavalry 1797 and 2nd or Midland Norfolk Yeomanry Cavalry from 1804. Promoted Brigadier General and briefly commanded all Norfolk volunteer infantry in 1804 before posting to Liverpool.

Burroughs, James B: Of Norwich. Divisional lieutenant of five hundreds in east Norfolk in 1803, jointly with the Reverend Mr Benjamin Salmon, but died same year. Raised and commanded Blofield & South Walsham Yeomanry Cavalry from 1795.

79

Buxton, Robert John: 1753/1839. Of Shadwell Lodge near Thetford. Tory MP for Thetford to 1796. Considered standing for county in 1796 in opposition to Coke. Later obtained a seat at Great Bedwyn in Wiltshire but left Parliament finally in 1806. Baronet 1800. Divisional lieutenant for three hundreds in south Norfolk in 1803.

Chad, Charles: Commanded 3rd Western Battalion of Norfolk Local Militia in 1810. Presumed relation of Sir George Chad of Thursford.

Coke, Thomas William: 1752/1842. Of Holkham. Largest landowner in Norfolk. County MP 1776/1784 and 1790/1832 except for short break 1806/7. Later created Earl of Leicester. Foxite Whig. Famous as "Coke of Norfolk" as agriculturist and stockbreeder. Raised and commanded Holkham Yeomanry Cavalry recruited from his tenants in 1798 (reluctantly) and again (with more enthusiasm) in 1803.

Coldham, James: Of Anmer. Divisional lieutenant of three hundreds in west Norfolk 1803 jointly with Sir Martin Folkes. High Sheriff of Norfolk 1809. Second in command of Eleventh Norfolk Volunteer Infantry.

Dillingham, Brampton Gurdon: Of Letton. Born c. 1740. High Sheriff of Norfolk 1789. Assumed name Dillingham as heir to Theophilus Dillingham of Shelton, Beds. Patron of Sir John Soane who designed his new house at Letton. Had Parliamentary ambitions. Chairman of the committee raising the county defence fund in 1794. Raised Hingham Yeomanry in that year but was too "aged and infirm" to be active commander.

Everard, Edward: 1761/1829. Partner in Edward Everard & Sons, a major firm of Lynn general merchants and shipowners. Alderman and three times mayor of Lynn. Commanded Lynn Volunteer Infantry from 1794 which unit later redesignated 1st Battalion Norfolk Volunteer Infantry.

Folkes, Sir Martin Browne, baronet: 1749/1821. Of Hillington. MP for King's Lynn 1790 to 1821. Served as deputy lieutenant and as an officer in the Norfolk Rangers. Divisional lieutenant of three hundreds in west Norfolk 1803 jointly with James Coldham.

Gould, William: Former regular officer of the line. Commanded Yarmouth Volunteer Infantry which was later redesignated 6th Battalion Norfolk Volunteer Infantry. Later commanded 3rd Eastern Battalion of Norfolk Local Militia.

Hamond, Anthony: 1742/1822. Of Westacre. Major landowner in west of county. High Sheriff of Norfolk 1792. Strong Whig and supporter of

Coke. Raised and commanded firstly Westacre volunteers in 1803 and subsequently 11th Battalion Norfolk Volunteer Infantry from 1804 (Freebridge Lynn & Smithdon) to its demise in 1806.

Harbord, Edward: 1781/1834. Younger brother of the Hon William. MP for Great Yarmouth 1806/12. Lieutenant colonel in his brother's volunteer regiment from 1803. Succeeded his brother as Lord Suffield in 1821 on the latter's death without children.

Harbord, the Hon William Assheton: 1766/1821. Of Blickling and Gunton. Married Caroline Hobart, daughter of 2nd earl of Buckingham. Divisional lieutenant for three hundreds in north-east Norfolk in 1803. Lord Lieutenant of Norfolk from 1807. MP for constituencies outside Norfolk 1790-96 and 1807-10. Succeeded his father, Sir Harbord Harbord, as Baron Suffield in 1810. Raised and commanded Norfolk Fencible Cavalry 1794/1800. Raised and commanded Blickling & Gunton Riflemen from 1803. Commanded 1st Eastern Battalion of Norfolk Local Militia from 1808.

Hare, Thomas: Of Stow Bardolph. Son of Thomas Leigh of Iver, Bucks and grandson of a London merchant who married a Hare. Assumed surname Hare by Act of Parliament in 1791. Had frustrated Parliamentary ambitions in 1797 & 1802. In 1796 he actually canvassed for a county seat but did not proceed while in 1802 he withdrew in favour of Wodehouse. High Sheriff of Norfolk 1803. Baronet 1818. Died 1834. Captain in Norfolk Rangers 1794. Raised and commanded Clackclose Hundred (Downham) Yeomanry in 1796.

Harvey, Charles: 1756/1843. Of Norwich. Lawyer. Brother of Robert and John. Recorder of Norwich 1801/1826. MP for Norwich 1812/1818. Served in Norwich Volunteer Infantry as lieutenant colonel. Inherited Stisted Hall in Essex from his maternal uncle and changed his name to Savill Onley.

Harvey, John: Of Norwich and later Thorpe Park. 1755/1842. Woolmerchant, manufacturer. Mayor of Norwich 1792. Keen horseman who revived racing on Mousehold Heath. Commanded Norwich Light Horse from 1799, in succession to his elder brother Robert, and later 3rd or East Norfolk Yeomanry Cavalry vice Colonel Money. Colonel commandant from 1824. High Sheriff of Norfolk 1825.

Harvey, Robert: 1753/1820. Of Norwich and later of Catton and later Stoke Holy Cross. Son and grandson of Norwich mayors. Mayor himself in 1787. Woolmerchant and banker. A leader of Norwich Tory party with Parliamentary ambitions. Served in East Norfolk militia in 1790s.

Commander of Norwich Light Horse from its formation in 1797. Transferred to become second in command of 3rd Norfolk Militia 1799. Raised and commanded 7th Battalion Norfolk Volunteer Infantry from 1803 to 1808 (Norwich).

Hobart, the Hon Henry: 1738/1799. Of Intwood. Fourth son of first earl of Buckinghamshire. MP for Norwich 1786-99. Pittite. His father was lord lieutenant of Norfolk 1745/56 and a nephew was Secretary of State for War and Colonies 1801/04. MP for Norwich 1786/99. Hobarts were an old Norfolk family but by the 1790s few were resident in the county. Captain in 3rd Norfolk Militia 1797 and its colonel 1798/99.

Hulton, Thomas : Heir to Isaac Preston of Beeston, assuming surname Preston in 1805. Baronet 1815. Formerly a militia captain, he became colonel of the 3rd Norfolk Militia in 1799 in succession to Henry Hobart. From 1804 commanded Norfolk 5th Volunteer Battalion (Aylsham area). Died 1823.

Ives, Jeremiah: 1753/1820. Of Catton Hall. From a Norwich family which supplied several mayors. Himself mayor of Norwich 1786 and 1801. Brother-in-law of Robert Harvey. Raised and commanded Catton Sharpshooters from 1803.

Jervis, John: 1735/1823. Admiral of the Fleet, Earl of St Vincent. Commander of Channel Fleet in 1799/1800 and again in 1806/7. First Lord of the Admiralty under the Addington administration 1801/1804. MP for Great Yarmouth 1784.

Jodrell, Henry: c.1750/1814. Of Bayfield. Barrister. Recorder of Yarmouth 1792/1813. MP for Yarmouth 1796/1802. Divisional lieutenant of four hundreds in north Norfolk in 1803 jointly with Sir Jacob Astley.

Keppel, William, fourth earl of Albemarle: 1772/1849. Of Quidenham. Lieutenant Colonel of West Norfolk Militia 1793/1799.

Kerrick, John: Of Harleston. A Thomas Kerrick of Geldestone (father?) was High Sheriff of Norfolk in 1788. Divisional lieutenant of two hundreds in south Norfolk 1803. Commanded Harleston Volunteers in 1803 and 8th Battalion Norfolk Volunteer Infantry (Loddon area) 1804/1806.

Lacon, Edmund Knowles: 1780/1839. From Yarmouth brewing family. Mayor of Yarmouth 1807. MP for Yarmouth 1812/1818. Succeeded his father as second baronet in 1820. Commanded Yarmouth Yeomanry Cavalry from 1803 to 1820 or later.

Loftus, William: Of Stiffkey. Died c.1831. Son-in-law of Lord Townshend. Regular officer. MP for Yarmouth in Townshend interest 1796/1802 and again 1812/1818. Already colonel when he raised the 24th Light Dragoons, a cavalry regiment, in 1794. Promoted major general in 1796 and general in 1813.

Mingay, James: 1752/1812. Of New Place, Thetford . His father was a Thetford surgeon and his brother became mayor. Made a fortune at the bar with earnings rumoured to be £5,000 a year.

Money, John: c.1742/1817. Of Crown Point, Norwich. Long career in the regular army. Also in Belgian insurgent army 1790 and French army in 1792. On Eastern Region staff from 1804. Commanded 3rd or Eastern Norfolk Cavalry from 1804 to 1807 and all Eastern Region voluntary cavalry from 1804.

Ottley, Robert William: Ex regular soldier who commanded the Swaffham Volunteer Infantry from 1803 and the 10th Battalion Norfolk Volunteer Infantry (Swaffham area) from 1804.

Patteson, John: 1755/1833. Originally heir to woolmerchanting firm and later proprietor of Norwich brewery. Mayor of Norwich 1788. MP for Minehead 1802-1806 and for Norwich 1806-1812. Had house in Surrey Street and estates at Colney & Bawburgh. President Norwich Union from 1812. Became impoverished in later years after financial failure. Founder and commander of Norwich Loyal Military Association 1797. Commanded Norwich Battalion of Volunteer Infantry 1803-1806 and 2nd Eastern Battalion of Norfolk Local Militia from 1808.

Petre, John: Of Suffield. Brother-in-law of the Hon William Asshcton Harbord. Commanded the 1st Western Battalion of Norfolk Local Militia from 1808. Born John Varlo, he adopted the name Petre, the surname of his maternal grandfather. Presumably a relation of Lord Petre of Essex and perhaps of John Berney Petre who lived at Westwick.

Pratt, Edward R: Of Ryston. High Sheriff of Norfolk 1793. Divisional lieutenant of three hundreds in west Norfolk in 1803. Unsuccessful Whig candidate for a county seat in 1817 following the death of his brother-in-law Sir Jacob Astley. Died 1838.

Styleman, Henry: Of Snettisham. Son of the Reverend Armine Styleman of Hunstanton Hall, and grandson of Nicholas Styleman of Snettisham, heir via his wife to the L'Estranges of Hunstanton. High Sheriff of Norfolk 1804. Raised and commanded Smithdon & Brothercross Yeomanry Cavalry from 1798 and Smithdon Volunteer Infantry from 1803. Died 1819.

Taylor, Joseph: Lynn merchant and shipowner. Founding partner of Gurneys Bank, Lynn branch. Lynn alderman and three times mayor. Raised and commanded Freebridge Lynn Cavalry, later Lynn Legion, from 1798.

Townshend, Charles: 1728/1810. Of Honingham. First cousin of the first marquess. MP for Yarmouth 1756/1796. Created Lord Bayning 1797.

Townshend, Charles Vere: 1785/1853. Grandson of the first marquess. Sometime MP for Tamworth. Commanded Norfolk Rangers (1st Norfolk Yeomanry Cavalry) from 1808.

Townshend, George: 1724/1808. Of Rainham Hall. Eldest son of third viscount Townshend, inheriting the title in 1764. Active career as regular soldier 1745/1762. Lord Lieutenant of Ireland 1767/1772. Master General of Ordnance 1772/82. Promoted major general in 1761; lieutenant general in 1770; general in 1782; and field marshall in 1796. Created marquess in 1787. Numerous other honours. Lord Lieutenant of Norfolk from 1792 until his death. Raised and commanded Norfolk Rangers in 1782 and revived the same unit in 1794.

Walpole, the Hon George: 1758/1835. Younger son of Lord Walpole of Wolterton. Regular soldier 1777 to 1797. As local major general he defeated a rebellion in Jamaica but a scandal over the terms of the truce he negotiated brought his military career to an end. MP 1797-1820 for Derby and then Dungarven. Foxite Whig holding minor government post 1806/7. Major commanding Aylsham Volunteers 1803/4.

Walpole, the Hon Horatio: 1752/1822. Son of Lord Walpole of Wolterton and in 1809 inherited from him the recreated title of earl of Orford. MP for Lynn 1784/1809. Supported duke of Portland's Whig government in 1790s. Lieutenant Colonel East Norfolk Militia 1780. Colonel of West Norfolk Militia 1792-1809.

Walpole, Horatio junior: 1783/1858. Son of Hon Horatio above, and inherited title of earl of Orford from him in 1822. MP for Lynn 1809/1822. In diplomatic service to 1815. Colonel of West Norfolk Militia from 1822 until his death.

Wilson, Robert: Of Didlington & Ashwellthorpe. A famous falconer and horsebreeder. High Sheriff of Norfolk 1802. Commanded South Greenhoe Yeomanry 1803 and was second-in-command of 2nd Norfolk Yeomanry Cavalry 1804/1820. Died 1828.

Windham, Rt Hon William: 1750/1810. Of Felbrigg. MP for Norwich to 1802 and subsequently for pocket boroughs. Originally a Foxite Whig he changed allegiances to support Pitt after war broke out, becoming Secretary at War. Out of office during the Addington and subsequent Pitt administrations, he became Secretary of State for War and the Colonies as part of the "All the Talents" administration of 1806/7. Raised and commanded Felbrigg Volunteer Infantry from 1803. From 1804 nominally commanded Norfolk 4th Volunteer Battalion (Cromer area) although harsh critic of the volunteer movement.

Wodehouse, Edmund: nephew of Lord Wodehouse. MP for Norfolk from 1817. Commanded Wymondham Yeomanry in 1803. After a spell as captain in East Norfolk Militia commanded 2nd Western Battalion of Norfolk Local Militia from 1810.

Wodehouse, Sir John, baronet: 1741/1834. Of Kimberley. Tory MP for Norfolk 1784/1797. Created Baron Wodehouse of Kimberley in 1797. Divisional lieutenant for three hundreds in central Norfolk in 1803.

Wodehouse, the Hon John: 1770/1846. Eldest son of John, first Baron Wodehouse. Tory MP for Great Bedwyn 1796/1802 and Marlborough 1818/1826. Unsuccessful parliamentary candidate for county in 1802 and 1806 in fiercely disputed elections. Succeeded his father as second Baron Wodehouse in 1834. Colonel of East Norfolk Militia 1792/1815.

Woodward, Thomas Jenks: Possibly the Mr Woodward of Bungay considered as parliamentary candidate for Norwich in 1806. Commanded 9th Battalion Norfolk Volunteer Infantry (Diss area) from 1804.

APPENDIX 3

NOTE ON SOURCES

PRIMARY

Major sources for information relating to the government of the county and the volunteers and, to a lesser extent, the militia have been the two local newspapers, the *Norfolk Chronicle* and the *Norwich Mercury*, more particularly the former and a summary of it for the early nineteenth century edited by the proprietor Charles Mackie published as *Norfolk Annals*, Volume 1 (Norfolk, 1901). Equally important for both militia and volunteers have been the letters from the lord lieutenant of the county to the Home Secretary in the Public Record Office (HO50 series) These contain not only large quantities of purely routine requests for appointment and promotion of officers and unit returns but nuggets such as Money's letters on artillery and his personal position, Bulwer's complaints regarding the treatment of any forces under his command and Robert Harvey's perennial and circumstantial gripes about not being promoted to full colonel.

The Public Record Office also contains much other information on all types of military organisation or activity in or affecting Norfolk. In particular PRO 30/8 (Chatham papers) 244 & 259 to 298 (miscellaneous, chiefly volunteers); HO42/37 and 50/26 (internal disturbances); WO30/56 (route plans), /58 (staff appreciation,1794), /67 (Reynolds report on Eastern District, 1797), & /100 (Byrne and Craig reports, 1803/4); and WO68/123 (digest of service by East Norfolk militia), & /467(Enrolment book of West Norfolk militia). The PRO library collection of Army Lists and special returns has been of particular value in constructing Appendix 1. More information on the movements of the militia regiments is to be found in the order book of the West Norfolk Militia (M39) held in the museum of the Royal Norfolk Regiment in Norwich.

Relevant material in the Norfolk Record Office is rather widely distributed amongst family and estate papers but includes some Townshend correspondence MS2658(3A3), MS2663(3A3), MS4493(55x7), MS5363 (5B6) & MS6258(5B4); the papers of the vicar of Stow Bardolph concerning censuses and plans for evacuation in 1803 MC379/9; the reports of Lieutenant Colonel Metzner from his inspection of the volunteers in 1803 MS67(T131A); and county returns of volunteer units and strengths for 1798 and 1799 MS5364(5B6). Amongst the estate papers the Hamond (HMN 4/)and Folkes (MC50) correspondence have been the most rewarding, but there is some material also under Wodehouse of Kimberly (KIM), under Bulwer (BUL), under Patteson (MC2015) and under Ketton Cremer (WKC).

The library at the University of East Anglia holds copies of General Money's two magnificent pamphlets, *Major-General Money's letter to the Deputy Lieutenants and Magistrates of the County of Norfolk on the present alarming situation of the country; and An address to the Norfolk Farmers and persons of all descriptions capable of bearing arms.* Neither pamphlet is dated but internal evidence suggests late July or very early August 1803. The local studies section of the Norfolk County Library at Norwich also holds copies of these and several other pamphlets by or about Money.

SECONDARY

There is a concise and clear account of Napoleon's invasion plans and Britain's countermeasures in Richard Glover, *Britain at Bay* (London, 1973) which includes a collection of transcribed documents from both British and French (translated) military and naval sources. There was intense interest in the history of the volunteers in the first decade of this century at the time of the Haldane reforms and the debates over the future of the army and whether it or its reserve forces should be based on conscription or volunteering. This brought forth a large crop of books and pamphlets. Harold Baker, *The Territorial Force* (London, 1909) is chiefly concerned with the legal and statutory background. Cecil Sebag-Montifiore, *A History of the Volunteer Forces* (London, 1908) puts the case for the volunteers eloquently and with patriotic fervour. However John Fortescue, *The County Lieutenancies and the Army 1803-1814* (London, 1909) is based on the most thorough research using particularly the correspondence between lords lieutenant and the Home Secretary (now PRO HO50 series). Fortescue, the great historian of the British Army, was tolerant of the militia but was convinced that the volunteers were a massive and wasteful diversion of resources which should have been employed in building up the regular army.

The only historian who in recent years has taken an overall look at British volunteer movements over several centuries is I.F.W. Beckett whose *The Amateur Military Tradition, 1558-1945* (Manchester 1991), based on an earlier thesis, includes chapters on each of the two French wars between 1793 and 1815. His chapter on the second of these wars draws heavily on Fortescue though differing in his conclusions. J.R. Western, *The English Militia in the Eighteenth Century* (London, 1965) is concerned chiefly with the national politics underlying the changing status of the militia. J.E. Cookson, "The English Volunteer Movement of the French Wars, 1793-1815", *Historical Journal* 32 (1989) pp.867-891 and Chapter 7 of Linda Colley, *Britons* (London, 1992) both contain interesting reflections on the motives for volunteering (or not). However the outstanding and most comprehensive work in recent years on the militia and the volunteers during the period covered by this work is J.E. Cookson, *The British Armed Nation 1793-1815*, (Oxford, 1997).

Little has been published specifically devoted to Norfolk although R. Hindry Mason had also seen the correspondence from the lord lieutenants to the Home Secretary (now PRO HO50 series) and incorporated some details concerning the county, including a summary of the divisional returns for

1803, into his *The History of Norfolk* (London, 1884). R.W. Ketton-Cremer, "Norfolk and the Threat of Invasion" in his own *Norfolk Portraits* (London, 1944) based on earlier articles in the *Eastern Daily Press* is almost entirely concerned with William Windham of Felbrigg and his efforts in the summer of 1803 to raise local volunteers on his own plan of an armed peasantry. J.R Harvey, *Records of the Norfolk Yeomanry Cavalry* (London, 1908) relies for the earliest period on correspondence then held by the Folkes family of Hillington, now in the Norfolk Record Office. Between 1794 and 1815 his work is based principally on newspaper reports and annual army lists of officers although he had access also to certain pamphlets not now available while he too had seen some of the correspondence from the lord lieutenant or had taken details from Mason.

Peter Kent, *Fortifications of East Anglia*, (Lavenham, 1988) provides a comprehensive account of the few fortifications as were already in or were constructed in Norfolk during the period. C.B. Jewson, *The Jacobin City* (Glasgow, 1975) is most useful for Norwich politics. Norfolk politics, MPs and elections are dealt with in detail for each constituency in R.G. Thorne, *History of Parliament – The Commons – 1790-1820* (London, 1986). David Ewart's *The Volunteer Movement in Norfolk During the French Revolutionary War 1793-1802* (unpublished University of East Anglia MA dissertation, 1998) is of considerable value for the first phase of the war, concentrating on the origins and social background of the volunteers, both officers and men.

Tim Carew, *The Royal Norfolk Regiment* (London, 1967) Chapter 2 gives summary information regarding the early history of what became Norfolk's own regular regiment. More detail, including some account of the Norfolk militia regiments, is provided by F Loraine Petre, *History of the Norfolk Regiment*, (Norwich, 1918) who in turn quotes Sir Charles Harvey, *The History of the 4th Battalion Norfolk Regiment late East Norfolk Militia* (1899). F.C. Hitchcock, "The Resusitation of Early Cavalry Regiments", *Cavalry Journal* 31 (1941) pp.107-116 gives the only account found of the 24th Dragoons raised by General Loftus. The economics of raising regiments are dealt with in T.H. McGuffin, "The Short Life and Sudden Death of an English Regiment of Foot", *The Journal of the Society for Army Historical Research* 33 (1955) pp. 16-25, an article about the 113th Foot, a regiment raised and then disbanded in a similar fashion to Bulwer's 106th.

Index

The place names Norfolk, Norwich, Yarmouth and King's Lynn are so common in the text that an index entry would be of little value. Entries for other place names within Norfolk, whether hundreds or townships, include references to yeomanry or volunteer units raised there. Most place names outside Norfolk are omitted.